Romain Rolland

SELECTED LETTERS OF
Romain Rolland

Edited by
FRANCIS DORÉ
and
MARIE-LAURE PRÉVOST

With a Foreword by
KAPILA VATSYAYAN

INDIRA GANDHI NATIONAL CENTRE FOR THE ARTS
DELHI
OXFORD UNIVERSITY PRESS
BOMBAY CALCUTTA MADRAS
1990

Oxford University Press, Walton Street, Oxford OX2 6DP

NEW YORK TORONTO
DELHI BOMBAY CALCUTTA MADRAS KARACHI
PETALING JAYA SINGAPORE HONG KONG TOKYO
NAIROBI DAR ES SALAAM
MELBOURNE AUCKLAND
and associates in
BERLIN IBADAN

SBN 0 19 562551 X

Phototypeset at Taj Services Ltd., Noida, U.P.
printed at Rekha Printers Pvt. Ltd., New Delhi 110020
and published by Ş. K. Mookerjee, Oxford University Press
YMCA Library Building, Jai Singh Road, New Delhi 110001

FOREWORD

Romain Rolland, musician, biographer, novelist, social activist, Nobel Laureate, committed in life and art to non-violence and peace, evoked reverence from all for the nobility of his character and the integrity of his art. Identified with humanitarian causes, the heroes of his biographies and his novels are idealists, filled with a passion to create bridges of communication between one age and another, the world of ideas of the West with those of the East.

In a preface to *Jean Christophe*, he said:

> I was isolated . . . I was stiffling in a world morally inimical to me. I wanted air. I wanted to react against unhealthy civilisation, against ideas corrupted by a sham elite.

Through the character of Jean Christophe, Romain Rolland, who reveals the past and the present, leaves the future open. The pristine absolute integrity of his search was shared by others, both peers and contemporaries, especially Tolstoy and Gandhi. Romain Rolland began as a researcher of Scarlatti and gained recognition as a renowned art historian of the 17th century. The social ethical being in him was sensitive, impassioned, and active. The eight plays inspired by the French Revolution commenced his twin journey as creative writer and a man committed to act by the values he cherished.

Biographies were his logical instrument. Beginning with Beethoven and Michelangelo, he explored the life of Ramakrishna and Vivekananda. In a preface to the biography *Prophets of New India*, (the life of Ramakrishna and Vivekananda) he voiced his opposition to the so-called two antithetical forms of spirit for which the West and the East are wrongly supposed to stand, and he asserted that 'there is neither East nor West for the naked soul.' To his Eastern readers, he said:

> At this distance from their differences I refuse to see the dust of

battle; at this distance the hedges between the fields melt into an immense expanse. I can only see the same river, a majestic '*chemin qui marche*' in the words of our Pascal. And it is because Ramakrishna more fully than any other man not only conceived, but realized in himself the total Unity of this river of God, open to all rivers and all streams, that I have given him my love; and I have drawn a little of his sacred water to slake the great thirst of the world.

To his western readers, he asserted:

> I have dedicated my whole life to the reconciliation of mankind. I have striven to bring it about among the peoples of Europe, especially between those two great western peoples who are brethren and yet enemies. For the last ten years I have been attempting the same task for the West and the East. . . In our days an absurd separation has been made between these two halves of the soul, and it is presumed that they are incompatible. The only incompatibility lies in the narrowness of view which those who erroneously claim to be their representatives share in common.

He went on to add:

> I belong to a land of rivers. I love them as if they were living creatures, and I understand why my ancestors offered them oblations of wine and milk. Now of all rivers the most sacred is that which gushes out eternally from the depths of the soul, from its rocks and sands and glaciers. Therein lies primeval Force and that is what I call religion. Everything belongs to this river of the Soul, flowing from the dark unplumbed reservoir of our being down the inevitable slope to the Ocean of the conscious, realized and mastered Being. And just as the water condenses and rises in vapour from the sea to the clouds of the sky to fill again the reservoir of the rivers, the cycles of creation proceed in uninterrupted succession. From the source to the sea, from the sea to the source everything consists of the same Energy, of the Being without beginning and without end. It matters not to me whether the Being be called God (and which God?) or Force (and what Force?). It may equally be called Matter, but what manner of matter is it when it includes the forces of the Spirit? Words, words, nothing but words! Unity, living and not abstract, is the essence of it all. And it is that which I adore, and it is that which

the great believers and the great agonostics, who carry it within them consciously or unconsciously, alike adore.

The letters chosen for the present volume, reflect the concern and commitment to the discovery and articulation of the phenomenon of polyphony—unity, in life and art.

Coomaraswamy had asserted 'Philosophy Perennius'. Romain Rolland asserted 'Aere Perennius'.

Addressed to a wide range of correspondents from Leo Tolstoy to Albert Schweitzer, Paul Seippel, Pastor Louis Ferriere, and Barbusse, the theme of 'oppressive violence of human society as it exists at present', is the unifying thread. Each letter is incisive, razor sharp, even irreverent to much that was happening around. In one impetuous letter to Leo Tolstoy, he questions Tolstoy: 'Why do you condemn art? Why, on the contrary, do you not use art as the most perfect means for realizing your renunciation?' He answers the rhetorical question himself by making the communication between art, life and death. In the same letter, he asks Tolstoy the question: 'You supress death and maintain life, which is of value, only because death has no hold on it; why not suppress both death and life together? Now, Art gives me this—the death of death—Why therefore would ecstasy, rather than empty action, not be the supreme state of wellbeing?' Rolland travelled inward to other dimensions. The correspondence with Nehru, Rabindranath Tagore and Gandhi represents this gradual transition, from intensity to a quiet fluid probing into the nature of man, the creative process and the place of the socially responsible citizen in the modern world, along with an inner life of reflection.

At no time was he an ivory tower intellectual. He was concerned not just to create art, but how to live his life. And it became even more apparent in his later equally impassioned stance against the rising tide of Nazism in Europe and in support of the Indian struggle for independence. One can see, both from a list of his correspondents as also from the contents of his letters, that Romain Rolland was himself engaged in and was drawn to others engaged in the pursuit of inner sources and resources that could be a beacon for action. Even in these few letters, all of the major movements and issues of the last decades of the 19th century and the first four decades of the 20th century are laid before us. The image of the river continues to be the guiding spirit of the pursuit.

The letters reveal Rolland's deepest perceptions of the arts, and a delicacy of inter-personal sensitivity, that is profoundly moving. After reading only a small selection of these letters, one feels one has touched the man; just as it is clear that the man had touched and been touched by those with whom he was corresponding.

The Indira Gandhi National Centre for the Arts (IGNCA), committed to integrating life and art and placing art and artistic creation in the context of life and related to social action, has chosen as one amongst its various programmes to reprint or translate works of writers, scholars, creative artists from all parts of the world who have searched for perennial sources and who have created bridges of communication between and amongst diverse traditions, civilizations, cultures, and different orders of time—the path finders. A. K. Coomaraswamy's thematically rearranged work is the centre of this programme. The first volume of the Selected Letters of A. K. Coomaraswamy reflects these concerns and commitments from one vantage point. The Selected Letters of Romain Rolland is the second in the series of letters of men of vision and reflection, creativity an socially responsible action.

It is appropriate that the exhibition on Romain Rolland and Gandhi concluding the Festival of India in January 1990 should be housed in the Gandhi Smriti where Gandhiji breathed his last, and also that it should include a reconstruction of the room in Villeneuve where the two men met and from which many of the letters included here were written. The Indira Gandhi National Centre for the Arts is proud to be able to offer this volume in conjunction with this occassion.

KAPILA VATSYAYAN

January 1990

PREFACE

Sixty years ago, in January of 1930, Romain Rolland noted in his *Diary* that the publication of his *Life of Vivekananda and the Universal Gospel* coincided with the Declaration of Independence of India by Gandhi and Nehru at the Opening ceremonies of the Congress of Lahore.[1]

This selection of letters of Romain Rolland, presented on the occasion of this double anniversary, and at the close of the Festival of France in India, recalls the privileged dialogue between India and the French writer. Attentive to the messages of other cultures, Rolland assigned himself the role of 'a sort of archway linking together the minds of men and women, of peoples and races' (letter 44), and particularly between Asia and Europe.

The *Voyage intérieur*, much like the interior voyage that the author took in his letters and writings, allows us a glimpse into the background of Romain Rolland's encounter with India.

Born in the small town of Clamecy, 29 January 1866, 'a pure provincial Frenchman, from the heart of the country', Rolland's interest in India began long before his first active engagement with the country from 1915 on.

A fervent admirer of Hugo, the young student at the Ecole Normale Supérieure read translations of Burnouf's *Bhagavad Gita* and the works of Spinoza, 'our European Krishna'. Called 'the musical Buddha of a revolutionary mysticism' by one of his fellow students, Rolland composed a notebook of readings on *Le Bouddha Siddartha*. Around the same time, with his comrades, he discovered the geography of India in the classroom of Vidal de La Blache, and among his papers is a programme for a concert of Oriental music held in 1889. Despite the advice of Ernest Renan, he did not pursue the

[1] Romain Rolland, *Inde*, p. 267.

study of an Oriental language, although he later strongly encouraged others to do so.

In Rome, Romain Rolland met Malwida von Meysenbug, whose influence was decisive; she shared his interest in India and had known J. C. Chatterji with whom Romain Rolland would exchange letters in 1931.

In 1892, Rolland married Clotilde Bréal. Her father, the philologist Michel Bréal, professor at the Collège de France, was the author of an *Etude sur la parenté des religions orientales*. Rolland also maintained a lifelong friendship with his sister-in-law, Louise Guieysse, who would found the *Nouvelles de l'Inde* and preside over an Association of the Friends of Gandhi.

India is also present in his earliest writings, in a theatrical project for *Aërt* dated 1896; in the manuscript of *Danton* which bears an epigraphic extract from the *Baghavata Purana*; and in 1897, the young writer contemplated a dramatic poem inspired by *Sakountala*.

In a folder entitled *Sagesse*, containing loose notes for *Jean-Christophe*, there is a mention of the *Bhagavad Gita*, and we know the remarks of Olivier to Jean-Christophe: 'The West is burning . . . I see other lights rising, from the depths of the Orient.'[2]

The first direct exchanges between India and Romain Rolland date, however, from 1915. While reading the illustrated pages of *the Arts and Crafts of India and Ceylon* by A. Coomaraswamy, he noted in his *Diary* with rapture, 'This universe is too rich, too full. . . . If I am accorded another ten or twenty years of life, I would like to lead western throughout onto these high plateaux, to places it has never even dreamt of.'[3]

From this moment, in fact, dates Romain Rolland's determination to discover and promote oriental culture in all its forms: artistic, intellectual, religious, political, and to foster through the strength of his own contagious sympathy, a veritable communion between eastern and western thought.

[2] *Romain Rolland, Jean Christophe, Dans la Maison.*
[3] Romain Rolland, *Inde*, p. 11.

The letters assembled here testify to his commitment: the sense of the spiritual unity of the world, the affirmation of a humanism that transcends boundaries: 'my country is anywhere, wherever there are men' (letter 17); reflections on the independence of the Spirit, on non-violence, fascism; and rising above the immediate problems of political action the hope of participating in the construction of the 'future cathedral of humanity' (letter 50) because 'The man of pure thought has no more than a weak effect on the present; his forecasts have only a long-term chance of working themselves out' (letter 45).

Francis Doré
Marie-Laure Prévost

ACKNOWLEDGEMENTS

Our most sincere thanks go to Lokenath Battacharya to whom this volume owes a large debt, for his translation of letters 2, 3,4, 5, 8, 12, 13, 14, 16, 17, 23, 25, 26, 27, 29, 35, 38, 39, 41, 43, 47, 48, 49, 50, 53, 54, 58.

Richard A. Francis kindly authorized the reprinting of his translations of letters 15, 16, 20, 21, 22, 23, 28, 30, 32, 34, 37, 40, 44, 45, 46, 51, 52, 53, 55, 56, 57, 59, 60 (*Romain Rolland and Gandhi Correspondence*).

We would like to thank the following editors who kindly granted permission for the publication of certain letters: Albin Michel (*Cahiers Romain rolland*); the Director of Publications Division of the Ministry of Information and Broadcasting, Government of India (*Romain Rolland and Gandhi Correspondence*, New Delhi, 1976); KTO Press (*Earth: a History*, New York, 1977: letter 1): Selwyn and Blount Topical (*I will not rest*, London, n.d.: letters 9–10); Visva-Bharati (*Rolland and Tagore*, Calcutta, 1945: letters 6, 7, 11, 18, 19, 24, 31, 33, 36, 61, 62); and *Prabuddha Bharata* (letter 42).

We would like to thank the Comité Administratif du Fonds Romain Rolland and its President Bernard Duchatelet, as well as the Chancellerie des Universités de Paris and the Bibliothèque Nationale for authorizing the release of the previously unpublished letters 8, 12, 17, 27, 35, 41, 48, 50.

The photographs of Romain Rolland with Rabindranath Tagore and Mahatma Gandhi appear courtesy Rod Schlemmer.

CONTENTS

ILLUSTRATIONS

THE LETTERS

To Leo Tolstoy

16 April, 1887

Monsieur le Comte,

I should not dare write to you if I had to express only my passionate admiration for your works; it seems to me that I know you too well through your novels to send banal compliments, which your great spirit scorns, and which would really be impertinent on the part of a boy, such as I. But I am impelled by a burning desire to know how to live my life; and from you alone I can expect a reply, for you alone have asked the questions which bother me. I am tortured by the idea of death, which I find in almost every page of your novels; I could not begin to tell you how your *Ivan Illitch* aroused my intimate thoughts; I shall not even try; I do not wish you to think that you are dealing with an ordinary flatterer, who writes only for the sake of writing to you and to try and get a few lines in your handwriting.—I swear that I am very sincere in writing to you about the powerful philosophical interest which your books excite in me.

I am convinced that social life, everyday life, is not true life, since it ends in death. Life can be good only if we suppress death. The reality of life is in the complete renunciation of the egotistical opposition of the living to death; it is in our making ourselves a living part of the 'Unique' Life. Let us suppress the end with the fusion of our existence in the universal being.

It truly seems to me, Sir, that is what you are saying; well, this thought is much the same as mine! I understand that, in order to succeed in renouncing one's personality, it is necessary to disminish as much as possible, and even to suppress entirely all individual consciousness, everything that can make us aware of our evil personality, our detestable ego. Your five spiritual rules for renunciation seem very sound to me, although I believe that for a Frenchman some other rules must be added. But that is of no consequence. Spiritual forms vary in different peoples. What interests me is the basis, the essence of your doctrine.—You claim that we should avoid vain affections, that we should work for everyone, not because of the love for mankind (that would be the equivalent of still more enlarging our ego, of inflating our soul with the passions of humanity), but because we are no longer willing to think, and because only beneficence, practical personal charity, physical work, will tear from us the deadly consciousness of our egotistical selves, and because charity alone will make us happy and will lead to ataraxy of thought, to the quiescence of the emotions.

Sir, I seek this effacement of myself, this healing ataraxy with my soul; I want it, and I believe that I can attain it; but why do you insist that it must be by manual labour? I shall ask you the question which is closest to my heart: Why do you condemn art? Why, on the contrary, do you not use art as the most perfect means for realizing your renunciation? I have just read, with great emotion, your latest work, *What is to be done?* The question of art is there put off to a later time. You say that you condemn art, but yet you do not give all the reasons for your judgment. Forgive me for not being able to wait any longer (I am young) and permit me to ask you for your reasons. I believed that I understood that, if you condemn art, it is because you see in it an egotistical desire for refined enjoyment, fitting only to increase our ego a hundredfold by refining our sensitivity to an extreme point. Alas! I know very well that, for most people and even for some artists, this is the purpose of art: an aristocratic sensualism, the sensualism of people whose perceptions have attained a rare delicacy. But is there not something else, Sir, something else which, for some people, is everything? And

that is precisely the forgetting of the personality, the death of
the individual so dissolved in sensations that he finally feels
nothing more, when the personality reaches the infinite
complexity which music for example has reached. No more
of oneself; no more memory; no more consciousness; a sea of
infinitely divided sensations. That is the state of ceasing to be;
that is the absorption in the One; that is ecstasy, the
hypnotism of hearing or sight, the hypnotism of the entire
spirit, so to speak. But do we not, by this path, reach the
ataraxy you spoke of? What can death do to us? We have
suppressed it, having ceased to exist even in this life.

I know what you will reproach me for: I am forgetting that
art is only a flower of evil, a crowning of all social injustice.
Some work and suffer in abject poverty so that I may remain
idle, as far as others are concerned, busy only with my own
happiness, which I could achieve just as well, if not better, by
manual work while promoting the well-being of others.—
But why should you expect me to act, work, and struggle for
my happiness and the happiness of others? After all, why
prolong this life? By working, I forget; but I still live, and I
cause others to live; I shall have children who will suffer like
me, until the time when, like me, they will understand that
happiness consists in forgetting, in no longer thinking. Why
not get it over with immediately? You suppress death and
maintain life, which is of value only because death has no
hold on it; why not suppress both death and life together?
Now, Art gives me this—the death of death.—Why therefore would ecstasy, rather than empty action, not be the
supreme state of well-being?

Oh! tell me, my dear Sir, whether you think that I am
wrong, and why. I do not see that you touch on this question
in any of your novels I am acquainted with. I am in love with
art, because it frees me from my wretched little personality,
because in art I am no longer anything more than these
infinite harmonies of sounds and colours, which dissolve
thought and suppress death. If I wished to work, to plough
the earth, I would still think. Consider that there are ancient

peoples who would not know how to reassume attitudes
forgotten centuries ago. Do you not believe that Art has a
great role to play, even in your doctrine, among those people
who are dying from the complexity of their civilization.

Please, my dear Sir, forgive this long letter; I know that
you are so kind that surely you will not be annoyed by it, and
that you will consent to clarify the doubts of a young
Frenchman who admires and loves you deeply.

Romain Rolland was at this time a student at the Ecole Normale Supérieur,
45, rue d'Ulm, Paris.

To Paul Seippel

23 April, 1914

Dear Friend,

I am not fully in agreement with you, on your definition of
France. I do not believe in a true France which is Germanic
and Gallic, and in a false France which is Roman and deforms
the former. The Latin element seems to me as essential and
necessary as the two others; and the true France is one which
harmonizes them. The superiority of one of the races over
the others does not seem to me established at all; and I am
radically opposed to those who, like Chamberlain (whose
work I know but do not like, the same way as I do not like
the works of Taine), become imperialist champions of a race
(questionable) and of a culture of a race. My mission (if I have
one) is every different: it is to work towards the unity of the
forces of the Occident, while waiting for the others.
Germanic and Gallic thought has as much need for Roman
imperial order as Roman thought is in need of the cheerful Gallic nature and Germanic idealism. (These definitions, I agree, are
much too simplified, but I am using them for convenience.)

The value of the renaissance of the Celto-Germanic spirit (evident, for thirty years, in French poetry and the other arts, like the Impressionist painting) is mainly as a reaction against the crushing domination of the classical spirit. But it should not crush that spirit in its turn; otherwise I would put myself on the other side of the boat to restore the balance.

I well see the great defects of the Latin mind in its art, notably in its rhetoric. But there is another side to every coin, and the defects of the Gallic mind (lack of seriousness, profligacy) and of the Germanic mind (lack of clarity, order and precision, false idealism, false depth, metaphysical muddle) are not less insufferable.

After all, d'Annunzio, who is one of the worst rhetoricians of today, is also one of the greatest poets; and I believe that some pages of his *Elegie Romane* will last as long as the Italian language. In any case, I woud exchange them for the entire French poetry of today. That does not prevent me from having an antipathy for the rest of his work; but it is enough already that the old Latin tree could spring up such branches.

How can you (excuse me for saying so) let yourself be led into this opposition of 'the great Romanesque art and the autochthonal Gothic' and of 'the Renaissance which ends in the impasse of academism and virtuosity'! There is more of virtuosity in the Gothic art of the 14th and the beginning of the 15th century than in all the architecture called classical or neo-classical. The great Latin spirit is a spirit essentially of virile reason and of sobriety of expression. Its rhetoric and virtuosity are only its degeneration, as they are also of the decadent Gothic art. This latter was dying when the Renaissance came; and had I lived then, I would have been one of the most fervent champions of the Renaissance. And then, what do you mean by 'autochthonal art'? Romanesque and Gothic art, full of elements imported from the East and the Far-East by invading races, who settled down on the land of the Gauls where the only autochthonal monuments were Gallic dolmens—and Roman monuments! Why should you have it that in Autun, for example, the cathedral alone should be the expression of the race, and not the Roman gates, the triumphal arches and the theatres? Is not Mistral as French as Lamartine? See how these two men, of so different races, loved and understood each other!

France is a harmony of races, or she is nothing. And the word Harmony, which is that of the dying Christophe, will always remain mine.

—No, I do not fear 'ethnic chaos', I invite it and work for it. I do not want the purity of filtered water or of rarefied life. I want first and foremost as much of life as possible and all the waters of the universe mingled in an immense river. The purity will come later, by itself; and pure or impure, I love my Loire as it is.

Affectionately yours,

To Seichi Narusé

23 May, 1915

My Young Friend of Far Away,

I thank you for your sympathy. I am happy that you could recognize a brother in Christophe.

You are right: the source of all art is life, life which is mysterious and profound, which penetrates and illumines the mind. But most of the artists (or false artists) of today come to a stop before the gate of life, and art is a plaything for them. The world-wide crisis which we are passing through, brings to light their futility. Very few, among the European élite, have resisted the folly of hatred. Yet this is a great age because of the heroism of the peoples; but it lacks spiritual leaders; it is a gigantic torso, without a head.

Continue, dear Seichi Narusé, with your efforts to master the European languages and thought, but let yourself be permeated with all that is great in the thought of Asia. We should now work towards pooling the wealth of the two worlds. Europe has as much need for Asia as Asia has for Europe,—I am sure of it. It is necessary that these two immense rivers should finally mingle their waters.

This year I am working in Geneva, at the International Agency, where I am attending to prisoners of war. I hope that next year we shall meet in Paris. My fixed address there is: 3 rue Boissonnade (XIVe).

Be of good courage! And be happy to live in a tragic age when humanity is renewing itself and when great tasks abound.

I shake hands with you cordially.

Your devoted,

I do not have a photograph handy. You will find one, though not a very good one, reproduced, I think, in the translation of Gilbert Cannan.

Written from the Hôtel Beauséjour-Champel, Geneva, Switzerland to Seichi Narusé, a Japanese friend.

To Amiya Chakravarty

18 March, 1917

Far-away Friend,

I thank you for your sympathy. I am happy that my *Jean-Christophe* has found so many echoes in your heart. To me it is one more proof of the universal fraternity of souls. This fraternity is something I believe in and I am working towards establishing a profound awareness of it among men of all nations, of all races. Most particularly, for the last few years, I have been feeling an urgent need to bring the spirit of Europe close to that of Asia. Neither the one nor the other is self-sufficient. They are the two hemispheres of thought. They have to be united. May that be the great mission of the coming age! If I were younger, I would dedicate myself totally to that task. I content myself with the joy of tasting in advance the plenitude of the future civilization, which will realize the union of the two halves of the human soul. I admire your Rabindranath Tagore because in him I already feel some resonance of that harmony. May my eyes (like my mind) drink some day this light of India which I see through your lines when you describe the light which surrounds you!

To Pastor Louis Ferrière

4 July, 1917

Dear Sir,

I read your letter with an affectionate emotion. If you were near me at this moment, I think I would have given you a kiss.

Nothing touches me more than an expression of fellow-feeling exchanged between two men whose thinking is different and, on certain points, even opposed. I am almost more sensitive to it than to the sympathy existing between two companions of the same thought and action. Because I feel in the former that fraternity in God which has always appeared to me as the highest ideal on earth. We have between us profound differences. They lie, mainly, I think, in the observation of facts.

I think that in the present war there is an enormous power of idealism on one hand, and on the other, a monstrous power of materialism, wickedness, ambition, mean and murderous interests (and folly, of course). You think so too.

The great difference between us is that for me, these two forces confronting each other, do not correspond to a division of Europe (and of the world) in two camps and I see the *Enemy* everywhere,—here more brutal perhaps, but there more hypocritical, and no less menacing, on one side as on the other.

I have known 'the Fair on the market-place' too well in times of peace, not to find it there again in times of war, in all countries,—but a thousand times more dangerous, because it holds in its hands the sword and the gag of the '*Salus Publica*' and a domesticated press.

I am not a pacifist because of weakness, who is fearful of the dangers of war. For the last three years I too have been waging a war, and it is not without danger. I am with those in spirit who condemn and fight against the iniquities of the imperial Germany.

But it is not because they are of Germany, it is because they are iniquities. And if I see iniquity elsewhere, I will not tolerate it more.

And now, I do see it elsewhere. I see it in the whole of the civilization of Europe (and of America), in the politics of all States, in the social system; and the worst of iniquities, it seems to me, is to fight against only one of them, while glorifying the others, when it is against all of them that one must fight.

I think I have written this once to your nephew Adolphe— I do not see Europe (the world) divided like this, by barriers:

I see it divided like this, by superimposed layers:

_____

_____

_____

_____

Everywhere there are men of good will,—and there are the others. Instead of playing the game of the latter, by pitting the former against each other, I aspire to make a union of all men of good will. They are in all nations and, in all of them, equally oppressed. You cannot be sufficiently aware of it if

you read only the Swiss dailies or those authorized in
Switzerland by the belligerent governments: because they
can say, or wish to say, only one part of the truth. But
someone, like me, who has been receiving for the last three
years the confidence of so many oppressed people, can hear
the cry of suffering and revolt rising from the entire world.
And I say: sooner or later, you too will hear it, because it will
explode. Woe be to the world then! Because it will be
submerged in a fresh deluge of human suffering.

To Rabindranath Tagore

10 April, 1919

Dear Friend,

Certain free spirits, who feel the need of standing out
against the almost universal oppression and servitude of the
intellect, have conceived the project of a Declaration of
Independence of the Spirit, a copy of which I enclose. Would
you give us the honour of uniting your own name with ours?
It appears to me that our ideas are not out of harmony with
yours. We have already received the consent of Henri
Barbusse, of Paul Signac, the painter, of Dr Frederik van
Eeden, of Professor Georg Fr Nicolaï, of Henry van de
Velde, of Stefan Zweig; and we expect the consent of
Bertrand Russell, Selma Lagerlöf, Upton Sinclair, Benedetto
Croce, and others. We think of collecting at first three or four
signatories for each country,—if possible, one writer, one
savant, one artist,—and then publish the Declaration, mak-
ing the appeal chiefly to the intellectual elite of all the nations.
If you can recruit for us some names in India, Japan and
China, I should be very much obliged. I could wish that
henceforth the intellect of Asia might take a more and more
regular part in the manifestation of the thought of Europe.
My dream will be that one day we may see the union of these

two hemispheres of the Spirit; and I admire you for having contributed towards this more than anyone else. Allow me to tell you in conclusion, how dear to us are your wisdom and your art, and accept, I pray, the expression of my profound affection.

I have allowed myself to make use of certain passages in your lecture of 1916 at Tokyo, in one of my articles published during the war. I am sending it to you under separate cover, with the request that you will pardon the imperfect translation. I enclose a little brochure dedicated to an ancient sage of Europe who has exercised great attraction over my thoughts and whom perhaps you will love also—Empedocles of Agrigentum.

Declaration of Independence of the Spirit

Toilers of the spirit, companions, scattered all over the world, separated from one another for five years by armies, by censorship and hate of nations at war, we take this opportunity, when barriers are falling and frontiers are re-opening, of making an appeal to you to re-form your fraternal union,—but let it be a fresh union, firmer and stronger than the one which existed before.

The war has thrown our ranks into disarray. The majority of intellectuals have placed their science, their art and their mind at the service of States. We do not wish to accuse or reproach anybody. We know the weakness of individual souls and the elemental strength of great collective currents: the latter have in an instant swept away the former, as no provision had been made for resisting. Let this experience at least serve us for the future!

And first of all, let us take note of the disasters that have resulted from the almost total abdication of the intelligence of the world and its voluntary subjection to the forces let loose. To the pestilence which is corroding Europe in body and spirit, thinkers and artists have added an incalculable amount of poisoned hate; they have searched in the arsenal of their knowledge, their memory and their imagination for old and new reasons, historical, scientific, logical and poetic reasons, for hating; they have laboured to destroy love and under-standing between men. And in so doing they have disfigur-ed, dishonoured, debased and degraded Thought, whose ambassadors they were. They have made it an instrument of passions and (perhaps without knowing it) of the egotistic interests of a social or political clan, of a state, of a country or of a class. And now from this savage struggle, from which all the warring nations, victorious and vanquished, are emerg-ing bruised, impoverished and in their heart of hearts (though they do not admit it to themselves) ashamed and humiliated at their orgy of madness, Thought emerges fallen with them, compromised by their conflict.

Arise! Let us extricate the spirit from these compromises, these humiliating alliances, this secret slavery! The spirit is the servant of none. It is we who are servants of the spirit. We have no other master. We are born to bear its torch, to defend it, to rally round it all those who have strayed. Our part, our duty is to maintain a fixed point, to point out the polar star, amidst the whirl of passions in the night. Amongst these passions of pride and mutual destruction, we shall choose none; we shall reject all. We serve Truth alone which is free, with no frontiers, with no limits, with no prejudices of race or caste. Of course we shall not dissociate ourselves from the interests of Humanity! We shall work for it, but for it *as a whole*. We do not recognize nations. We recognize the People—one and universal,—the People who suffer, who struggle, who fall and rise again, and who ever march forward on the rough road, drenched with their sweat and their blood,—the People comprising all men, all equally our brothers. And it is in order to make them, like ourselves, aware of this fraternity, that we raise above their blind battles the Arch of Alliance, of the Free Spirit, one and manifold, eternal.

R.R. was writing from Villeneuve (Vaud), Hotel Byron, Switzerland.

To Rabindranath Tagore

26 August, 1919

Dear Sir,

I was glad to receive your friendly letter, dated 24 June, and two of your books which were sent by your publisher, Macmillan: *Nationalism* and *The Home and the World*. I cordially thank you for them. The reading of *Nationalism* has been a great joy for me; for I entirely agree with your thoughts, and I love them even more now that I have heard them expressed by you with this noble and harmonious wisdom which—being your own—is so dear to us. It gives me profound pain (and, I might say, remorse, If I did not consider myself a human being rather than a European) when I consider the monstrous abuses which Europe makes of her power, this havoc of the universe, the destruction and debasement of so much material and moral wealth of the greatest forces on earth which it would have been in her interest to defend and to make strong by uniting them to her own. The time has come to react. It is not only a question of justice, it is a question of saving humanity.

After the disaster of this shameful world war which marked Europe's failure, it has become evident that Europe alone cannot save herself. Her thought is in need of Asia's thought, just as the latter has profited from contact with European thought. These are the two hemispheres of the brain of mankind. It is necessary to re-establish their union and their healthy development.

More than once have I thought of a review of Asia and Europe (of course including America under European civilization) which would bring to light the moral wealth of these fraternal and inimical worlds. It would not concern itself with politics, but with the treasures of thought, of art, of science, and of faith. Everything would be pooled in common. I do not think it would be difficult to find in Europe an elite of writers and thinkers who would be interested in a review of this kind, published in several languages (two at least, English and French), and who would collaborate. Do you think that such a project is likely to find in Asia, in the most important centres of culture, the effective help which would be necessary?

This is only an idea, but one which I believe is latent in the minds of many today; and that is why I was so keen to speak to you about it. The day it will begin to be realized, the collaboration of the best European minds will not be lacking.

I had, last week, a visit from a Dutch friend, the great writer Frederik van Eeden, who has one of the noblest hearts and one of the purest consciences in Europe. He has for you an affectionate admiration. You were often in our conversations.

Believe, dear Sir, in my deepest affection,

I expect to remain in Switzerland till mid-October. I shall then come back to Paris, where my address is 3 rue Boissonade (XIVe.).

You have undoubtedly received a manifesto of the French group 'Clarté'. Through mistake my names appears in some lists among the members of the Committee. I have regard for Henri Barbusse and I admire him much as a writer; but I'd like to say that I am not a member of this group.

R.R. was writing from Schoenburnn-Bad (Zug) Switzerland.

To Hélène Claparède-Spir

27 April, 1921

Dear Madam,

Rabindranath Tagore has just spent a week in Paris. I have seen him frequently and we had long conversations together. He will be in Switzerland next Saturday or Sunday and has requested me to announce his arrival to friends in Geneva and Zurich. He would like to put forward in public a laudable project for an international university, which he is going to set up in India at Santiniketan, near Bolpur. At the moment he is travelling through Europe trying to generate interest in it among intellectual personalities of all countries. Unfortunately, the time he can spare for his stay in Switzerland is short; he can hardly stay there for more than ten (perhaps fifteen) days. Is it possible to organize, in this short time, a meeting in Geneva? I have just written on this subject to Seippel and M. H. Bodmer, so that they come to an understanding with Tagore about a meeting in Zurich.

Tagore is leaving Paris today for Strasbourg, where his address is: c/o Prof. Sylvain Lévi, University of Strasbourg. But I don't think you have the time to write to him there, if, as he intends, he has to be in Switzerland by Saturday. Immediately on his arrival in Switzerland, you could find out his address from Seippel and Bodmer (as he will begin by Zurich) and write to him or telephone him at once.

If it is not possible to organize a meeting so quickly, I think it is essential in any case that he is put in personal touch with some of the major personalities of French-speaking and German-speaking Switzerland; and I have no doubt that the Institute Jean-Jacques Rousseau would be of special interest to him.

I am sending you herewith a copy of his noble 'Appeal in favour of an international university'. As you will see, when you read it, (and during conversations, his thought is even clearer) it is less a matter of an institute of learned studies (though such work should have a place there) than a centre of great international spirit, where the thought of Europe and that of Asia could come closer and learn to know each other by what they have in them that is best and most human. So it is a work of faith, at least as much as a work of science. I need not tell you that I am entirely devoted to such ideas and that I will do all I can to help Tagore. You will, I am convinced, be very happy to know him. His personality is not less harmonious than his poetical work. His existence is a blessing, specially at a time like this.

Do remember me to Mr Edouard Claparède and please
believe, dear Madam, in the expression of my respectful
sympathy.

To H. BARBUSSE

14 December, 1921

My Dear Barbusse,

I have received your article, 'Concerning Rollandism'. I
thank you for the personal sympathy you there evince for
me, and the tone, so noble and so measured, that you have
brought to this controversy. I hope that we shall never depart
from it in the sequel; for happen what may, we shall always
be united against the forces of reaction—political, social,
moral, and intellectual; the more menacing they become, the
more united shall we be.

I do not intend, today, to send you a full and comprehen-
sive reply. The time at my disposal and the limits of an article
do not permit it. I shall do it at leisure, in the form of a
statement of my ideas and my faith. If I have abstained from
it till now, it was partly because you begged me not to
oppose your efforts; and you know that my intervention has
not been useless in the matter of the adhesion to *Clarté* of
some of the leaders of your foreign groups. Your courteous
attack on 'Rollandism' has led me to resolve to make my
position perfectly clear. Perhaps the result would be to found
a hitherto non-existent 'Rollandism'. I shall for my part
regret it, for I am averse to all that might contribute to
weaken individual initiative and the sense of liberty. It is not
in any case for the 'Rollandists', it is on behalf of Romain
Rolland alone, that I make a brief answer here.

You are surprised, my dear Barbusse, that I consistently
refuse to associate myself with your group for intellectual
action. As a matter of fact, from the inception of *Clarté*, I

have felt myself to be in disagreement with the spirit of its founders. I did not, however, wish to form a judgment about it off-handedly, and so I was obliged to take up an attitude of reserve and watchfulness.

Allow me to express my regret that you interpret that reserve as a 'detachment'—a retreat into the too famous 'ivory tower'.

Whoever knows me, whoever has read even one of my books, can say whether their tone is that of a 'detached' man, or rather on the contrary, of a man torn by the sufferings of the world and struggling to alleviate them. Whatever one may think of my ideas, it is difficult to deny me faith. That faith has, since my youth, supported me in my trials, and borne me across the gulf.

One of your friends, I believe, has called me 'a mystic *en disponibilité*'. Without considering the balance of diverse elements which constitutes my thought, this witticism, designed to be anything but agreeable to me, is nearer the truth than your reproach of 'aesthetic detachment'. But your friend deceives himself in thinking that this religious force (in the most liberal sense of the word) is of no use to mankind today. He had scarcely any notion (there is little diffidence amongst you) of the vast underground forces which are now accumulating in the spirit of humanity, and the powerful currents which are agitating its depths. Your attention is a little too restricted to the surface of the world; it rationalizes life excessively. And judging from what you said, the tendency of *Clarté* seemed to be to assimilate the enigma of human evolution to a problem in Euclidean geometry.

Excuse me for smiling in a friendly spirit when I read in your article that 'there cannot be any errors in calculation in this geometry of social revolution, which is defined and formulated by the general principles of *Clarté*'. What an abstract conception it is of man, of this fountain flowing with subconscious energy, and primitive forces, and cosmic radiance! More royalist than the king, you are more rationalist than those scientists of today with whom you compare yourself, and who themselves are far indeed from affirming the 'infallibility of fundamental laws'!

However that may be, my dear Barbusse, speaking for myself, I do not believe in it, in the *infallibility* of the laws of your 'social geometry'; and I will not rally round it:

1. Because, in theory (but in political and social matters, what is theory? Achievement is all)—in theory, the doctrine of the neo-Marxian Communism seems to me (under the absolutist form in which it is at present clothed) very little suited to the true progress of mankind.

(I will return to this later; the question is too general, too broad for one to pretend to deal with it in a few words).

2. Because, in fact its application in Russia has not only not been devoid of lamentable and cruel errors (for which the villainy of the associated bourgeois Governments of Europe and America carry the heaviest responsibility), but because to its application, the leaders of the new order have too often sacrificed, of set purpose, the highest moral values: humanity, liberty, and most precious of all, truth. On this matter, I shall have a great deal to say. We will come to it. It is unfortunately only too certain that for the majority of the leading spirits of the Russian revolution, as in the rest of Europe, everything is subordinate to *raison d'État*.

I do not oppose one *raison d'État* in favour of another. And militarism, police terror, or brutal force are not in my eyes sanctified because they are the instrument of a Communist dictatorship instead of being the instrument of a plutocracy.

I am sorry to hear you say that 'the intrusion of violence is but a detail, and a provisional detail'. For I think that a Minister of National Defence and of the Bourgeois Order would be able to employ the same formula. It is radically false in both cases. If it is to have any chance at all of being true, human nature must be as a 'clean slate', a blackboard on which you can scribble anything with a piece of chalk and then wipe it off with a sponge. But the living organism is made of an ultra-sensitive substance, in which the subtlest impressions are recorded; and violence leaves indelible traces on it. Let us admit it: in the actual revolutionary troops we find in fact in every country many independent ex-soldiers from the war 'for Justice and for Liberty'. The label has altered. There is nothing to show that it will not change once again. But the mentality is not less disturbing than it was before, for a new habit of violence has been superimposed on the old, and would inevitably predispose men to renewed and stronger violence in the future.

It is in that sense that I wrote in *Clérambault* (and I am more than ever of that opinion): 'It is not true that the end justifies the means. The means are even more important for true progress than the end. . . ' For the end (so rarely reached, and always incompletely) but modifies the external relations between men. The means, however, shape the mind of man according either to the rhythm of justice or to the rhythm of violence. And if it is according to the latter, no form of Government will ever prevent the oppression of the weak by the strong.

That is why I regard it as essential to defend moral values, more perhaps during a Revolution than in ordinary times, for Revolutions are moulting periods, when the spirit of the nation is more susceptible to change.

Besides, I believe firmly that the greatest service that you can render to the Communist cause is not to make an apology for it, but to criticise it frankly and truly. There is only one man in the party who exercises in all its fullness such independence of judgment: it is Lenin. But that vigorous dominator is himself limited by his doctrinairism and by the walls of the Kremlin, by which I mean his power. Around him I hardly see any but scribes of the law. Communists, be free men! Labour incessantly to correct your handiwork, by daring yourselves to point out its errors and fighting its abuses.

So long as I do not feel in a party this passion for truth, with its corollary, respect for free criticism; so long as I see nothing there expect the will to win at all costs, and by any means, and this confusion of the interests of the party with

absolute justice and good; in a word, so long as the spirit of
the servants of the Revolution remains narrowly political,
despising under the name of 'anarchism' or of 'sentimental-
ism' the sacred claims of the free conscience, I shall hold
myself aloof, without having any illusions as to the issue of
the conflict.

To hold oneself aloof does not mean to remain inactive. To
each his work. While you are striving (and I praise you for it)
to avert the most immediate dangers, I have the feeling that
the present convulsions of the world are but the beginnings
of a long crisis in the growth of humanity, of an era of
upheavals, during which the nations will have to suffer a
great many more attacks than those they have just experienced. We are arming ourselves for this age of iron, an age
our eyes will not see, but wherein, I hope, a little of our spirit
will survive. We are striving, on behalf of those who will
come after us, to save and concentrate the forces of reason, of
love, and of faith, which would help them to weather the
storm when, after having accomplished its labour of a day,
your Communist credo will succumb (excuse me for
anticipating it) compromised by the injustices of the struggle,
or undermined by the indifference which is the fate which
follows victories that are too exclusively political.

★ ★ ★ ★ ★

Do not misunderstand my thought. I admire, my dear
Barbusse, your courage, your ardour, and your chivalrous
loyalty. Our two lines of activity are not opposed. They are
complementary. We are both carried along by the same
revolutionary stream, or better, the stream of human
renovation, of perpetual renewal. Both of us have our eyes
turned towards the ascending light, and we both seek to
break the mortal coils of the past which hamper the march of
man. But I do not wish to substitute for them harsh new
bonds.

With you and the Revolutionaries, against the tyranny of

the past! With the oppressed of tomorrow, against the tyrants of tomorrow!

Schiller's phrase—it has always been by motto: *In Tyrannos*. (Against *all* tyrants.)

★ ★ ★ ★ ★

(I here add, as an appendix, an extract from a letter written in December, 1921, to a Russian revolutionary, where I insist upon the necessity of saving 'the moral values' during a Revolution):

'These moral values must always be safeguarded. In the interests of humanity, and in that of the Revolution itself. For a Revolution which neglects them is condemned, sooner or later, to much more than material defeat: to moral deterioration. "Victory at all costs" is a sorry policy for a Revolution. For the "at all costs" already deprives it of its best weapons: those of the spirit. And if it is vanquished, it has not only lost the battle, it has lost *everything*. Montesquieu's old phrase: Republics are founded on virtue, is more profound than it may seem. Certainly, they cannot maintain themselves save on a basis of religious respect for the human conscience and for truth. For if they are based only on force, on fraud, on falsehood, other regimes offer to the latter a great many more advantages: and force, fraud, and falsehood will conspire to ruin the Revolution which claims to retain them in its service. And when the supreme assault comes, where would the Revolution still find the resources of sacrifice without which it cannot subsist? . . .'

This is R. R.'s first open letter to Henri Barbusse in their controversy over the subject of 'Independence of Thought'.

To H. Barbusse

2 February, 1922

My Dear Barbusse,

I am sorry that in your rejoinder you have departed a little from the restraint I appreciated so much in your preceding article. To relegate amongst the bourgeoisie the interlocutor with whom one is in disagreement is a convenient procedure, but too forensic. We are not trying here to play on the chord of proletarian Chauvinism. (It is not worth any more than national chauvinism). We confront each other, Barbusse, bourgeois or not, two workers who owe all that they are solely to their own effort, two free men who have both purchased their liberty at the cost of hardships, and who seek, both of them, the truth. Nothing more. Nothing less.

What right have you to decree that whoever does not think as you do is outside the Revolution? The Revolution is not the property of a party. The Revolution is a mansion of all those who wish for a better and happier humanity. It is then, mine, too. Only, I do not wish to live there in an atmosphere of coterie, such as that which both bourgeoisie and Communists vie with each other in imposing on us. That is why I throw my windows open. I am even ready to break the glass panes, if necessary, to breathe. For there are some of us who make the claim (exorbitant as it may seem) of remaining within the Revolution, and of remaining there as free men.

I no longer speak for myself alone, as in my first letter. For in the controversy which has since developed, some of your friends have, like you, separated my cause from that of the Rollandists.

'To Rolland, Rollandism is permitted. To the Rollandists, it is not.' I do not accept these privileges. First of all, if they are accorded to me in consideration of the ordeals I have endured in the past, it is forgotten too much that others have endured the same ordeals, others have during the war fought against war, risked all their future for the cause of internationalism, and still suffer from the grave consequences of it all. But it is not a question here of privileges, it is a question of the right which belongs to everyone: the right of preserving one's freedom of thought unimpaired and entire.

For men of thought, this right is not only a right, it is a duty. For of what value is an idea, which begins by toeing the line, and so abdicates its position? Party ideas, Church ideas, caste ideas—the tools of every form of oppression! we know it but too well! For centuries the mind has been striving to tear off the bandage. One by one they fall: the bandage of the old theological and royalist Sorbonne; that of the modern secular and republican universities, of the *ancien régime* or of the Revolution, black, white, red, they are all alike, they are still all bandages. And our first duty is to repudiate them all.

★ ★ ★ ★ ★

You, Barbusse, feel the generous need for action, actions at all costs, so as to wrest the people from present miseries and those others, the even more agonising miseries with which the future threatens us. I love that spirit in you: and God forbid that I should say anything to discourage it.

As for me, I feel a different need: to see reality as it is, and not such as I desire it to be. A fine plan, nicely logical, is fine—on paper. But I look for the men for whom the plan is designed. Barbusse, outside you and a handful of others, I have not found them. The leading men in France, as you know, do not present a very reassuring sight. And amongst the masses, I see, surrounded by the enormous apathetic egoism of the great majority, violent and tortured forces calculated to destroy and to be destroyed much more than to construct. I have not the gift of self-delusion; I cannot say to myself, 'You have only to wish, and the world will be changed'. For I know that at present the world *does not want* to change.

The world, our Western Europe, is a great wounded beast; it is licking its wounds, and the blood continues to flow. Is it through new wounds that it is going to find its lost energy? I am afraid rather of its losing what little blood there may still be in it. It is exactly because I am aware of the epic potency of a great Revolution that I do not see in it a desperate remedy for nations that are exhausted and on the verge of convulsions. That is, I believe, the great psychological error committed by the highest revolutionary leaders of today. A Revolution, to be victorious, needs immense reserves of energy, store-houses filled to bursting with the robust health of a race and its joyous hopes. I cannot expect that from the eviscerated wolves which are the nations of Europe, and which prowl, bleeding (two or three of them, dying) across the devastated fields.

You accuse me of pessimism. But there is, to begin with, something worse, as Gustave Dupin said, than the pessimism which looks unblinkingly at reality; it is the mask of optimism which conceals the face and the scalding tears. (You, my revolutionary friend, whose name I shall not mention here, as you stiffened in your hard conviction, I have seen them, the tears, in your eyes. . . .)

No, Barbusse, I am no pessimist. For I have not set to my mind the narrow limits of the present or of the immediate future. History has accustomed me to embrace vaster spaces: I know that Paris was not built in a day, and that human unity will not be achieved in a century. I do not believe any the less in it. I even believe in it the more, since transient failures do not suffice to shake my faith. And without ever experiencing one single day of despair, I labour unceasingly for the accomplishment of our idea.

It is here that you are lying in wait for me, with your question as to the action I propose.

Our common enemy, Barbusse, is the oppressive violence of human society as it exists at present. But against that violence, you arm an adverse violence. In my view (I have said it and will not enlarge on it) that method only leads to mutual destruction. If you act against your enemies in the fashion of your enemies, as the Germans and the French did during the war, there might be at the end of the social war some treaty of Versailles, a paper victory. But in fact, it would be the ruin of all.

Let us grant that I am mistaken. There are, in any case, other weapons I claim to employ.

The first, on which I shall not dilate—for it is or ought to be the special weapon of intellectuals: we are that, you and I: and, before thinking of the duties of others, we must begin by discharging the duties of our profession—the first is the intrepid struggle of the spirit, of all the forces of enchained reason, to examine, check, and pass sentence, as our valiant friends of the Union of Democratic Control are doing, on the acts of those in authority; as well as ridiculing, castigating, flinging stones at abuses, in emulation of the steely criticism, the embittered irony of Voltaire and the Encyclopaedists who did more for the downfall of the monarchy than the handful of hot-heads who took the Bastille.

But there is another weapon, much more powerful and suited for all, to the humblest as well as to the most exalted: it has already proved its efficacy amongst other peoples, and it is astonishing that no one ever speaks of it in France: it is that employed, amongst Anglo-Saxons, by the thousands of 'conscientious objectors', that by means of which Gandhi is now undermining the domination of the British Empire in India—Civil Disobedience; I do not say passive resistance for, make no mistake, it is the supreme resistance. To refuse his assent and his collaboration with the criminal State is the most heroic act that can be performed by a man of our times; it requires of him, an individual, solitary in face of the colossal State which could strangle him, in cold blood, behind closed doors—it requires of him an energy and a spirit of sacrifie incomparably greater than he needs to face death whilst he mingles his breath and the sweating agony of his body with that of the herd. A moral force of this sort is not possible until it is aroused in the heart of men—of each man, individually; the fire of the conscience, the quasi-mystic sense of the divine which is in every being, and which, in the

decisive moments of history, has lifted great nations as high
as the very stars.

But that is what 'you do not sufficiently consider'. (To
repeat a phrase with some malice [friendly, I assure you!]
which you launched, without asking yourself if perchance
the lack of regard with which some of you have touched our
intimate beliefs might not have affected us, me and some of
my companions.) Too preoccupied with collective forces (of
which I know as well as anyone else the formidable
magnetism), you do not perhaps attach sufficient value to the
individual conscience, the isolated, the religiously isolated
and naked conscience, the lever of the world. The one
amongst you who sensed it most vividly was poor
Raymond-Lefebvre, your friend and mine who wished to
found a mystical cult based on the heroes of the Revolution.

But neither can that be the work of a day. The two great
factors in all profound human transformations are, first of all
(and here we are in agreement), *sacrifice*, which is the heroic
pattern of that transformation, accomplished by a man,
accomplished by ourselves; and in the second place, *time*, the
master mason who builds with the blood and the pain of
generations. How many generations of sacrifice, some of
them brilliant, most of them obscure, has it taken to found
on the indestructible ruins of Rome the new Christian world?
Do you think that the Revolution which is to establish
fraternal unity among human workers is of less importance,
that you should suppose it would require less delays on the
way to accomplishment?

Dear friends, do not hold it against me that I am older than
you in years, and believe less than you do in the achievements
of the near future. Your belief, in any case, is not greater than
mine in the duty of not losing a day in hastening its advent.
No, the attitude I recommend to my companions is not one
of detachment and renunciation. I say, quite on the contrary:
Never go to sleep. Never compromise. Never come to terms
with injustice and falsehood. Push aside, yourselves, one by
one, all the old gods, to make room for new ones (amongst

which 'Humanity' should not perhaps be the last!) Dare! Sacrifice yourselves. And rest assured your sufferings will not be in vain. You toil for the centuries to come. You must not complain that you are not nearing the end. Be glad that you have a share in a task that infinitely exceeds the duration of your life. That is a method of experiencing immortality in life.

★ ★ ★ ★ ★

I hear you, Barbusse, when you say: 'During these days France is dying and Europe is threatened'. Defend them, then! (Although I hear, too, the implacable voice of Nemesis, saying: 'Europe is paying for it. Justice must be accomplished!') But up to the last man must fight destiny. Fight, then, Barbusse. We shall fight with you, but as free men, for that which seems just to us, and against that which seems unjust.

We respect your faith, we admire your courage and valour. But do not compel us to believe in all that you believe, to do all that you do. It would not only be an intolerable exaction, but a grave political error to enforce within the ranks of the same cause the same duties on all men.

And in the last reckoning one of the best means of defending Europe and the future is still to do one's job well. If everyone was fighting, who would fill the barns? And what would the world emerging from your Revolution be worth if the scholars and the artists did not continue their researches, without yielding by a hair's breadth their ideals of truth and beauty to the new social dogmas, without even remembering that these dogmas have come into existence? For there is Barbusse, something beyond the humanity of a day, with its faiths, its griefs, and its ephemeral triumphs: it is the humanity of all time.

I address these words to my colleagues who write, to you above all who claim to be marching in the vanguard of thought:

Do you think that it is the present duty of the artist, the

scientist, and the man of thought to join, as in 1914, the army
of Justice; to join, as in 1922, the army of the Revolution? Or
does it not rather seem to you that the best way of serving the
cause of humanity and even of the Revolution is to protect
the integrity of your free thought—even if it be against the
Revolution, if the latter does not understand the vital need
for liberty? For, not understanding this need, the Revolution
would cease to be the fount of renewal: it would have
become but another and novel embodiment of the monster
with a hundred faces: Reaction.

★ ★ ★ ★ ★

PS. Two words more, Barbusse, on the subject of your
'social geometry'. You were irritated by my 'smile': there
was no malice in it. I know that a great artist like you will not
be cramped within the narrowness of a formula: I only
wished to put you on your guard against the dangers of the
one you had employed. And your renewed explanations do
not sufficiently avert the danger.

It is perfectly true to say, as you say, that 'what is fragile
and contingent are the metaphysical hypotheses which experimental science admits, but not the constant relations
which it establishes between their appearances'.

Yes; we only know, thanks to our sensations, relations,
which we call phenomena, for we do not judge, we do not
perceive, save in relation to a certain unity, a basis of
comparison, the choice of which indicates at what scale of
observation we place ourselves. Thus, science only knows
facts: and that knowledge, *at a given level*, is true.

But you seem to confuse these scientific facts with laws,
when you ascribe to the latter the verity of the former. To
deduce from facts a law is to superpose on a group of facts an
abstract construction which depends on fundamental
metaphysical hypotheses. In fact, to establish a law one
eliminates certain relations from a given totality, so as to
consider only the rest. And this elimination, which is not

arbitrary, which is legitimate, is none the less a function of our brain adding itself to the reality.

It is therefore false to say that 'whatever may be the prevailing theory on the essential nature of elements like space, time, or matter, the reality of the physical or chemical laws is not thereby affected'. The proof of it is that the law of gravitation and all the laws of physical energy have been modified by Einstein's theories. Do you say that this does not touch their *reality*? But what is the *reality* of laws? There are no laws in nature. It only offers us relations between facts; and the law proceeds from us, from us alone. If you think that natural laws have a concrete existence, in the book of nature, you are a mystic, Barbusse, without knowing it.

That is not the most serious thing. Here is the phrase which in your article immediately follows upon what I have just discussed, and brings your reasoning to a close:

'I have not said anything else but that, and I persist in affirming it, as well as the idea I have of the relations of identity between sociology and the other applied sciences.'

Here you begin by jumping at one bound from pure to applied science. And, again, you ascribe to the latter the truth which you attribute perhaps with too much confidence to the former.

Let us grant that physical laws (the most precise of all) fit in exactly with reality. While we are applying one of them, we regard as negligible all those movements in the field which do not depend on our law. We commit therefore one more abstraction, which is no doubt justified; but our applied law will be a law with a given approximation (not to mention experimental errors).

What am I to say when, taking a fresh jump, we pass with you from the physical and chemical sciences to sociology? If physical and chemical laws are themselves extremely difficult to apply to living creatures in isolation, how could one apply them to colonies of living creatures, where the psychological element plays a enormous role, a role which we are yet incapable of determining? One does not have in sociology any but *laws of frequency*, rough approximations. And the only mathematical laws that one could at present apply to them are those of the calculus of probabilities!

We are far from 'social geometry'!

I conclude, my dear Barbusse, that you are a man of faith. Coming from my mouth, the judgment is certainly not a criticism. I also am a man of faith. For good or ill our gods are tied to the chariot of the Republic. Yours, if I mistake not, is called Equality. And mine, Liberty. 'They are both powerful gods', as the old woman said, in Racine. They do not always get on well together. Let us endeavour to bring them into harmony. And whether they agree or not, let us shake hands!

This is R.R.'s second open letter to Henri Barbusse in their controversy over the subject of 'Independence of thought', written from Paris.

To Rabindranath Tagore

7 May, 1922

Dear and Great Friend,

If I have not written to you since our last meeting in Paris, you have not been therefore any the less often with me. Across the bounds of space, where speech is needless, I feel the concord of our thoughts.

I had great pleasure in seeing last month several times one of your young disciples, Mr Kalida Nag. I like his quick and vibrating intelligence, the sacred fire which animates him, and the fervent admiration with which he speaks of you. He has to take part in some international conferences which will be held in August at Varese, in the north of Italy, and which are organized by the International League of Women for Peace and Liberty (my sister is one of its

secretaries). Bertrand Russell, Georges Duhamel, Count
Kessler, perhaps Gorki, will gather there together; I shall
most probably spend a few days with them.

It is my ardent hope to see you again, sooner or later, in
India and to co-operate, in my humble way, in your great
work of mutual understanding. One of the principal obstacles is that I do not speak English and that your students do
not understand French. If however my presence could be
useful to you in some way, I should like to come and stay a
short while at Santiniketan. In any case it would not be this
year, but perhaps in the autumn or winter of 1923, provided
my rather delicate health permits me to do so. I should thus
realize one of the dreams of my life.

In the meanwhile, we are trying at Paris to start a French
review of wide international outlook, without any political
bias, wherein will fraternize not only the thought of the
various nations of Europe but wherein a large place will be
given to the thought of Asia. I do not know whether we shall
succeed in finding the necessary financial help. But in case, if,
as I hope, the magazine can be launched in the month of
October, I would ardently wish that you would honour our
first number by your name. I thought that perhaps you
would consent to let us publish in French translation some of
your letters from Europe, fragments of which I have seen in a
review published in the English language. They would have
for us a living interest. Will you kindly tell me if, in principle,
you would consent to it? Moreover, the young editors of the
review, my friends René Arcos and Paul Colin, will write to
you.

I have just left definitely my Paris rooms and have installed
myself in a little Swiss house, on the border of Lake Leman,
near the Savoy Alps. I could no longer bear the moral and
material atmosphere of Paris, the perennial trepidation of
streets and souls. I had to live there a long time, but only by
enveloping myself in my own music and my own dreams. I
believe I have now earned the right to withdraw from the
vortex of men in order to be near the heart of Man. Here I

have silence, the murmur of trees and of waves breaking on the sands, the breath of prairies and of pure white glaciers.

I wish you happy days of harmony. May you experience some tender joy in knowing the pious affection which I have for you!

Your devoted friend,

I thank you for the beautiful photograph which you sent me through Mr Kalidas Nag. I shall permit myself to send you next one or two of my latest photographs.

Written from Villeneuve (Vaud), Villa Olga, Switzerland.

To the French Association of Friends of the Orient

6 June, 1922

I thank you for your kindness in writing to me and for sending me your Bulletin of Friends of the Orient. Recently, at the Bossard bookshop, I looked through its first number with lively interest; and I had great pleasure in reading your excellent moral report of June 1921. I congratulate you heartily on your efforts to fight the 'colonial spirit' and establish in France the high Asian culture, which should be one of the foundations of the renewed European mind. On that, I feel in perfect agreement with you. My only regret (which, between us, I am taking the liberty of telling you frankly) is about the very pronounced official political character of the Association which the composition of its honorary committee gives to it. I am always on my guard when free intelligence is mexed mixed with politics (of whatever kind); and in that, I am perhaps, at heart, half Indian, in the sense of my very dear friend R. Tagore. *Timeo Danaos.* . . .

Pray believe in my cordial sentiments.

Written to Association Française des Amis de l'Orient.

To Kalidas Nag

17 June, 1922

Dear Mr Kalidas Nag,

Affectionate thanks for your kind letter and for the copy of the letter of Tagore.

I need not tell you what joy I experienced in the expression of sympathy from Tagore, he who is so dear to me. I could reply employing almost the same terms as he has used. No poet or thinker of today's Europe, I feel, is as near to me at heart and in spirit as he is. Which proves the vanity of those artificial divisions established between the thought of India and that of the West. For what am I, if not a pure Frenchman by race, a provincial coming from the centre of the country, belonging to a family which for centuries has been free of any mixing of foreign element in it, confined until my fifteenth year to the narrow horizon of my small town in the region of Nevers, and since then, absorbed in my life of thought, without any personal contact with Asia until very recently, nor having much connection even with the other countries of Europe? And yet, it has been, in my solitary soul, like a vibration of humanity, profound and fraternal, which rising from the innermost being, has gradually spread, reaching step by step Germany, then Russia, then India—and even beyond India, the souls of the Far East—and bathing myself completely in its great waters of harmony. Of course, I still know very little of the immense thought of your India. But what I can certify is that never, at any moment, in whatever I have read or learnt of it, have I felt myself a stranger. Its words have always responded to my most fundamental intuitions and aspirations. Nothing of it was new to me, it was a rediscovery. It was like my own treasure which I had left burried and was now finding again. Moreover, I was struck by the affinity of Indian thought with that of the great souls of Greece, or of Europe of all the ages, which was my normal sustenance. The only difference, I think, is that the substance which the Indian thinkers had was richer: they thought of the same thing, but they thought it more thoroughly, more comprehensively also, taking all the aspects into account—in short, with the magical coating of more splendid forms. Depth, breadth, splendour, they are the essence of the Indian genius. But the same thought, always. *Our* thought. I could recognize it well.

How is it then that so few from our West recognize it the way I do? Why do they even appear to misapprehend it, reject it, brush it aside with distrust and antipathy, be afraid of it? *Because they are afraid of themselves*, because they do not want to see into the very depths of their soul. I have the impression that the European, for a long time, has forced on himself, to use a modern term of psycho-analysis, a terrible 'repression', which is heroic perhaps, but inhuman, in order that nothing should stand in the way of his will to act and dominate. Off and on, the man cracks; the gods, repressed, bound and famished, escape through the cracks and become wild demons, smashing and looting everything; then, a more powerful will puts them back in their cage. But each time, the edifice is shaken a little more. Today, I feel it verges on its ruin. That is why the Europeans, dimly intuitive of the fact, tremble and turn their eyes away from the fathomless ocean lashing against the walls of their tower. But I, who was gasping for breath inside the tower, have come out of it (I have even had the door slammed behind my back), and I am taking a new lease of life, thanks to the breath of this ocean.

I am not surprised at the very hard battles that Tagore must wage in his own country. To tell you the truth, I am not at all sure, like him, that our thought will end by conquering (or by convincing) in our lifetime. But I am so much imbued with faith in infinite life that the era of our humanity seems to me but one episode in the eternal cycle. Its duration is (has to be) too brief to allow the Being to accomplish any great progress in a conclusive manner. Everything remains (and is meant to remain) in a state of rough outlines. We are sketching out the great work. Other humanities, in other universes, will no doubt continue it and bring it to its finish. I am not impatient. As Christophe, while dying, dreams: 'You will be reborn. Rest! . . . '

We have the time. . . .

* * * * *

I do not want to bother Tagore with these thoughts, which he must be familiar with. But if you think that some of them can be of interest to him, do convey them to him, please.

I do hope we shall have the pleasure of seeing you this summer, for a little longer. If I cannot come to Varese myself, I am counting on it that you will stop, on your way, at Villeneuve. Maybe Gabriel Monod-Herzen will be accompanying you during the journey. That would make me doubly happy. I have much affection for this young friend, who seems to have in him a harmonious blending of the high qualities of purity and liberty from his double race.

I have taken the liberty of giving your address to my friend, the poet René Arcos, who is trying at the moment to start a magazine in France, of truly 'panhuman' spirit, outside of all parties. He would have the collaboration of the best French writers of liberal thinking, and I would wish that Tagore would let him publish in it the translation of some of his works, notably his letters from Europe, which should generate great interest. Your personal collaboration in it would also have been much desired. But judging by the latest news, I fear that Arcos may not succeed in finding a publisher, nor the necessary financial support. Money is never lacking for magazines which are nationalistic, capitalistic, or simply fashionable, 'demi-mondaines'—or, more accurately, street-walkers. But it is impossible now to find money in France for a disinterested thought which seeks to unite men. Europe falls, like a stone.

Goodbye, dear Kalidas Nag. I send my cordial and friendly greetings, along with remembrances from my sister.

Your devoted,

An affectionate handshake from me to the Herzens, father and son.

Written from Villa Olga, Villeneuve (Vaud), Switzerland.

To Dilip Kumar Roy

                                                    31 July, 1922

My Dear D. K. Roy,

My sister has already written to you that we will be very
happy to listen to you in Varese, that you can give your
lecture in English, on whatever subject as you may like to
indicate, and that the normal duration of each lecture is about
an hour. Today, we received a telephone call from Geneva
saying that your name was properly registered on the list of
lecturers—barring a notification to the contrary from your
side.

For any additional information relating to the stay in
Varese etc., please correspond, not with me, but (in English)
with Miss Emily G. Balch, General Secretary, International
League of Women for Peace and Liberty, 6 rue du Vieux
Collège, Geneva.

★ ★ ★ ★ ★

Now, let me reply briefly to some of your questions.

You have asked me if I could secure for you an audience
which would be receptive to Indian music and capable of
appreciating it.

My dear D. K. Roy, when I write something, I never
bother to ask myself whether it will find a public who will
understand and appreciate it. Had I asked myself such a
question, I would have thrown away my pen, as I am all too
certain that no one really understands the art and the thought
of another person. A reader takes what suits him, what he
wants beforehand (if need be, he even invents it), and he

leaves the rest. My *Jean Christophe*, which has been read by thousands of readers, has aroused in them impressions and impulses of all sorts. But there has not been one single reader among them who has espoused my thought. That is impossible. And the great creators know it well. When Wagner thought of writing his *Tristan*, do you know the audience, he had in mind? He wrote in for a *Brazilian** audience, because that public there *did not know him* and, consequently, was for him a fancied, ideal public. He could dream that the public of his dream would understand him. But he knew well that none of the audiences he knew— European audiences—would ever understand him.

One does not write a work of art, one does not create, to impose one's thought. One creates, for *sowing*. All creation is a *generation*. The progenitor does not know the son who will come out of him. He diffuses life. His only concern should be that this life should be healthy. The rest does not depend on him.

If, therefore, you have in you thoughts which are beautiful and strong, pour them out open-handedly and do not ask whether the humanity which surrounds you is worthy of receiving them. It will be, know that for certain! Nothing is wasted in Nature. Of what you have sown (if the seed has been good), some shoots will always rise—some sparks will kindle—perhaps not immediately, nor in the souls one might have expected to be the most apt to take advantage of it—but sooner or later, here or there. One must have faith in the irresistible force of Life.

So much for the question in general. As to your particular question of Indian music, I affirm once again that there is nothing in it which should be inaccessible to the soul of a European musician. (In the same way I find nothing in your Indian thought which is essentially different from ours. Alas, for my avid and insatiable mind, it is still *not sufficiently*

* A proposal was made to him that he could give one of his works to the Opera of Rio de Janeiro.

different! I aspire to break the circle in which the human spirit goes round and round. . . But we shall discuss this later, some day.) You say that you have not found among the musicians of Europe an understanding of Indian melody. But who are the musicians of Europe you have known? I fear you may have had to deal almost exclusively with those proceeding from the system of the great Germano-Flemish harmonists and polyphonists, which has reigned over Western Europe since the 15th century and of which the German symphonists are the greatest personifications. It is but one of the forms of European music: it is essentially Germanic; and in my opinion, it is on its way out. Though Mediterranean Europe has been, and still is, under the powerful yoke of Harmony (which has become classic) emanating from Germany, it has known, and still knows, other musical systems which are much nearer to the melodic and polyrhythmic systems of Arabic and Indian Asia. If you visit Spain, you will find there everywhere forms which are still living and popular and which, in other western nations, were pushed back, during the middle ages, by modern polyphony. And I tell you again that among these medieval forms, Gregorian chant (as rediscovered by the Benedictines of Solesmes) is a pure melodic form (without any accompaniment and without bar) as rich and refined, and as perfect, as your Indian melodies. But perhaps you have never had occasion to hear it performed following the strict rule of the Benedictines of Solesmes, which the *Schola Cantorum* of Charles Bordes and Vincent d'Indy adopted in Paris. Because generally, in Germany or in England, they distort this chant by adding to it metres and accompaniments of modern harmonic music.

Lastly, I do not share at all your opinion that it is neither possible nor permissible to appreciate Indian music—(or any other great music)—without going to India and studying it assiduously on the spot, like a professional or an initiate. I believe that an art is great only when it can move even the most ignorant. Of course, not completely, nor exactly either.

But it is necessary that a great work has something in it to satisfy the spiritual hunger of all men. Let everyone find there something to drink and eat. 'Take it, for it is my blood,' as in the Christian Communion. Christ did not die only for a few catechumens. So why should you want a great artist to suffer, dream and create only for a few initiates? The illumination of beautiful song, like the inspired work, falls where it pleases God, not us. Our role is not to choose the elect. Our role is to sing.

In haste, and affectionately yours,

I hope to see you, on your way, between Lausanne and Brigue Domo Dossola. All along the Lake Geneva there is no lack of hotels; and from Vevey to Villeneuve, all this region is connected by a regular electric tramway. At Villeneuve, there is the Hotel Byron, which is very good, but quite expensive. For Veytaux-Chillon, near Territet, I would recommend to you the Hotel Richelieu, which I have found satisfactory in the past and where prices are more moderate.

Written to Dilip Kumar Roy from Villeneuve (Vaud), Villa Olga, Switzerland.

To Ganesan

August, 1922

. . . I profoundly admire Mahatma Gandhi, but I do not believe I can write the introduction which you ask of me. Truth to tell, with all due respect to the great man, my ideas differ somewhat from his on certain points. As far as I can gather from the extracts of his work which you sent me, he is less an internationalist (as I am) than an idealistic nationalist. I see in him the highest and purest type of spiritualized nationalism, a type which is unique today and which could be offered as a model to the egoistic and materialized nationalisms of present-day Europe. I intend to do this some day in an article in a European review, But I could not do it in an introduction to a book, for I should not be as free there to discuss his work and to show the points where I differ from him. May I add that there is nothing more contrary to my way of working than giving hasty opinions on such a considerable system of thought and action. I cannot be content with a superficial reading; I want to think about it at leisure. So forgive me if I decline the honour of writing a preface to M. G.'s volume; it is precisely because I have such a high regard for him that I do not want to talk about him other than after mature reflection and in complete liberty. (N.B. The proofs you sent me are without the introductory and closing pages; in any case I would never speak about a book before receiving and reading *the whole text*.)

To Kalidas Nag

8 February, 1923

Dear Friend,

I do not know how to thank you for the touble you have taken to reply to my sister's questions, and particularly, to copy out all these texts. I fear I have taken advantage of your extreme complaisance. But I am too selfish to regret it, for your information has been precious to me, and the letters of Tagore are admirable. These testimonies of the highest value are not only poetical (whatever Tagore writes has something aerial about it, it is a song of a 'prophetic bird', to use the title of a beautiful page of Schumann), but they are also for placing definitely a historic debate.

How beautiful this debate is! One does not know whom to admire more: the saint or the wise genius, What unique good fortune for India to have simultaneously in its possession these two great men, each representing one of the two faces of the highest truth!

I must admit, Nag, my friend, that I feel a little ashamed to think of you reading my pages on Gandhi. I'm so well aware of how impossible it is for a European to treat such a broad subject without going wrong! Even if I were to read everything there was to be read, I'd still lack the atmosphere created by India's religion, her education and her country. Forgive me in advance for the mistakes I shall make! At least there's one good thing, that you'll be able to read my article in two numbers of the review *Europe* (15 March and 15 April—I'll have them sent to you), and if you'd like to point out the necessary changes, I can improve my work for the volume of Gandhi's translated writings to which it is later to form the introduction. (I even hope to bring it out again, a little later on, as a small volume in my collection of 'Heroic Lives', like the *Beethoven* and the *Tolstoy*.)

There's no one more worthy of a place in this heroes' gallery. I know no hero more pure, more straightforward or more truthful. You can be proud to possess that 'great soul'; Europe has none approaching him—not by a long way! Despite reservations which one might make about some of his notions and their dangerous deformations in the minds of his disciples, I admire and venerate Gandhi.

But I expect to meet with a complete lack of understanding from my (so-called!) colleagues in Paris when they read my essay. Already Jean Bernier of *Clarté*, who must have got wind somehow of what I'm going to publish, has made a scornfully ironic reference in an article in the *Cahiers Idéalistes* to my admiration for Gandhi. As far as he's concerned, nothing to do with India is of any interest to Europe. (And he's an 'internationalist'.)

Isn't it mysterious, my dear brother, that whatever I read of the Indian thought appears to me so natural, so familiar, and nothing of what I think seems familiar to my country-men? Whether they praise me (which is rare), or criticize me, they always miss the point of what I have written or thought, of what I am. It will soon be time for my soul to set about finding its true milieu, as I have the feeling that in this incarnation I went tc the wrong house.

Tagore was gracious enough to give me, for the publishing house of Roniger, authorization to publish his novel *Gora* in French and German. And now Roniger must forgo this precious privilege because of current problems of publishing in German and Swiss-German, which prevent him from realizing this year the projected *Weltbibliothek*. I feel very vexed at this obstacle and tender my apologies to Tagore. I hope that at least the magazine *Europe* will be able to take advantage of one part of his authorization.

Good bye, dear friend. With our affectionate remembrances to you

Yours devotedly,

Could you tell me in which number of *Modern Review* Tagore's letters appeared, the ones of which you sent us copies?

Gandhi says he's a '*Sanatani*' Hindu; what does the word mean?

In the bloody riot of Chauri-Chaura, they talk of a *Thana* where policemen were burnt to death. Is it the name of a particular building?

(Don't be in a hurry to reply.)

It's quite some time since I had news of the Monod-Herzens. It's my fault, as I should have written to them, which I couldn't. I hope they are well. Do you know whether the father of Gabriel has found the publisher he was searching for, for his big work?

To Raimund Eberhard

15 February, 1923

Thank you affectionately, dear Mr Raimund Eberhard. It is at such moments that one must affirm, from one country to another, one's unshakable faith. Mine breaks away, increasingly, from the idea of nations. My country is everywhere, wherever there are men. And when one persecutes the other, I am always with the oppressed.

I am afraid this period of nations may have to follow its course till its completion, it is a phase of human evolution. Nation states which once were a great and useful realization of human progress, have now become a harmful superfluity and detrimental to progress. They will destroy themselves; and other organizations, broader, better adapted to the needs of the new humanity, will take their place.

Let us not have doubts about the future and let us give credit to time! Great social transformations are slow going. But nothing can stop them. There is no doubt whatsoever that, through all the current disasters, the world nevertheless is on its way towards unity. At the cost of what sufferings! But it seems that suffering is the law of all birth. The new humanity rends the belly of the humanity of old which carried it.

I am at present finishing quite a long essay on Mahatma Gandhi, the great apostle of non-violent action (because the word 'passive resistance' does not suit at all: the non-violence of Gandhi is the most powerful action, nothing can resist it). This study will appear simultaneously in a new French magazine, *Europe* (which will be of broad humanistic spirit), and in the *Friedenswarte* of Vienna which is going to reappear next month, under the direction of Rudolf Goldscheid. Try to procure a copy. I think you will be happy to know the life and thought of this admirable man. He is the greatest soul of our times. The master of us all.

Cordially yours,

Written from Villeneuve (Vaud), Villa Olga, Switzerland.

To Rabindranath Tagore

2 March, 1923

Dear Friend,

I thank you affectionately for granting me the authority to publish *Gora* in French. My sister will be glad to translate it from the English; and I intend to revise the translation. If there is any difficulty, I shall seek the advice of our friend Kalidas Nag.

But there is no longer any question of *Gora*'s appearing in that *Weltbibliothek* of which I spoke to you, and which was the project of a German-Swiss publisher, Emil Roniger. Since two or three months, political affairs between France and Germany have deteriorated so much that the German and Swiss-German publishing firms feel the effects. Emil Roniger has had to postpone his project.

So the question at present is: 1) to publish *Gora* in the review *Europe** which we have just started in Paris, and the first number of which is due to appear shortly. I am collaborating in it with Duhamel and other principal European writers, who feel like me that they are '*cives totius orbis*'; 2) to have it published by one of the big Parisian publishers, probably Stock, who would wish to publish, if possible, your big prose works, especially your novels. Kalidas Nag will no doubt write to you about this matter. You will kindly arrange your terms with the publisher, or let me know them, so that I may pass them on to him. I would only request you to remind him that you have chosen my sister and myself to be the translators of *Gora*.

I have just finished a pretty long essay on Mahatma Gandhi, based on the volume of collected articles in *Young India*. I shall have it published in the review *Europe* as well as

* I should have liked very much to find a title which unites Europe and Asia. Unfortunately, the beautiful name *Eurasia* is used in a too special sense; which is a great pity! It is wonderfully suggestive.

in several German and Russian reviews. Without subscribing to all the ideas of Gandhi, which appear to me somewhat too medieval, (especially in the case of his disciples, like Prof Kalelkar, whose *Gospel of Swadeshi* would confine India within the walls of a cloister), I have conceived for the man Gandhi himself and his great heart burning with love an infinite love and veneration. In a chapter of my Essay I have taken the liberty, according to your admirable essays already published, of recalling the position you have taken up with regard to Gandhi, and the noble debate of ideas which has beeen evoked between you. The highest human ideals are confronted therein. It seems as if it were a controversy between a St Paul and a Plato. But transported to India, its horizons have expanded. They embrace the whole earth, and the whole of humanity joins in this august 'Dispute' (in the serene sense given to this word by the famous fresco of Raphael in the Stanze of the Vatican). In my conclusion, I have shown you united in the feeling for the beauty (and even for the fruitful necessity) of the sacrifice of self through love.

It may gratify you to know that your thought is the nearest to mine that I actually feel in the world, and that the soul of India, as expressed by your luminous spirit and the ardent heart of Gandhi, is for me a larger native land, in which my limbs stretch themselves free from the bonds of fanatical Europe which has bruised them. But I know quite well that in India you also are isolated enough. (And I have an impression that it was a comfort even to Gandhi to be imprisoned.) We carry within ourselves our God and his free creation.

My sister wishes to be remembered kindly to you, and I beg you to believe in my devoted affection.

Will you have the kindness to arrange to send me the numbers of the *Modern Review* in which *Gora* has appeared?

Written from Villencuve (Vaud), Volla Olga, Switzerland.

To Rabindranath Tagore

11 June, 1923

Dear Friend,

We thank you cordially for your letter of 27 April and for sending your two novels as well as the '*Visava-Bharati*'. We have spent several evenings in the atmosphere of your thoughts,—my sister reading out to me your majestical *Vision of Indian History* and the charming story *Broken Ties*. As regards the longer story *The Friends*, we start reading it this evening.

The panoramic essay on Indian thought is full of grandeur. This is history illumined by an inner light,—the Soul of India that builds up her body and the ordered continuity of her movements and her actions.

As regards the story, it is exquisite. I cannot sufficiently admire the mischievous and tender humour, the suppleness and living smoothness of the story, the dialogue, and the attractive gifts of the narrator. My sister has translated it, and the review *Europe* is glad to publish it, since you have authorized us to do so. Do not doubt that it will not charm the European public. Your little Damini is a lovely sister of many of our young women in the West; and you do know how to read these feminine minds! Satish's uncle is a figure of unforgettable character; and he too would find in France some fellow-men of the same spiritual race, atheist-saints for whom even nothingness is a principle of joy and goodness. The excellent Srivilas Babu will be liked by every one. Only Satish is of a kind rather remote from Europeans, and a western narrator would probably have given more import-ance to the picturesque element of the Swami's dancing troupe which for you is undoubtedly almost a common sight. But your story is to me one more example of the unity of the human soul and its emotions, behind the diversity of customs. And as a work of art I particularly love the first part, the character of Damini in its entirety, the chaste and burning poetry of these loving souls, and so many profound things, so many emotions veiled behind the smile of a fugitive word (especially in the last part). Thank you for having allowed us to know them first, and for letting these pages be known in France, pages which bring you nearer to us and which therefore will win you the love of a greater number here.

We have spent the last month in Paris and in London. The occasion for my visit to the latter town was the first meeting of the international club of writers, founded by John Galsworthy, which has spread all over Europe,—without as yet achieving a benevolent and mutual comprehension which is Galsworthy's sincere aim. This has been an occasion for me to see my English colleagues at close quarters,—Thomas Hardy, Bernard Shaw, Zangwill, Wells and others. But I also had the good fortune of meeting in London your disciple and friend C. F. Andrews. Of the few hours we spent together I have kept a beautiful and pure remembrance: he has the soul of a true apostle of early times, transparent as crystal, modest, sincere and serene. Needless to tell you with what piety he spoke of you. He has provided me with precious documents to complete my study of Gandhi. We have also corresponded with W. W. Pearson with regard to *Gora*, which my sister will translate for the publisher Stock as soon as the English translation by Pearson is finished.

We count on seeing again this summer at Villeneuve both Andrews and Pearson. We also expect, by the end of July or in August, our dear Kalidas Nag who will soon leave us in order to rejoin you, after having indefatigably travelled across Europe from the north cape to Gibraltar. I have just read with great interest the thesis which he has successfully submitted to the Faculty of Letters at Paris, on *Artha Sastra*. In many passages his 'vision of history' is related to yours. But we were amused to realise that our glorious European diplomats were small boys compared with the astounding Kautilya and his disciples. 'Nothing new under the Sun', says our ancient proverb.

I hope you have received the three numbers of the magazine *Europe* which I have sent you, and where you will read my study on Mahatma Gandhi. I hope nothing will displease you in those pages which I have devoted to you. As regards the mistakes in my study, they were inevitable for a European, a novice as yet in his knowledge of India and her immense soul. I have done what I could. And if, as no doubt, I have not always understood correctly, I hope to have at least *felt* intuitively: for I have *loved*.

On the whole, the magazine *Europe* is of a good literary standing; its intentions are excellent; but I would like in it more air, more sun, vaster horizons. The best people in France have a little too much liking for the sheltered 'home' (a problem which is dealt with in one of the volumes of *Jean Christophe*), for the small beloved province, and are little inquisitive with regard to the outside. And at this moment the weariness of the war makes itself always felt. The soaring impulses have folded their wings and have withdrawn themselves into cages; they wait for the gale to blow over instead of hurling themselves into it and of rising higher. How much I regret not to be younger by twenty years!

It seems to me that there exists in Asia, here and there, a spiritual awakening which is both more lively and more pure than in Europe. For instance, in young Japan, I have been greatly struck when reading a beautiful religious drama by Kurata Hyakuzo, which has just been translated into English: *The Priest and his Disciples*. Do you know it? There hardly exists in Europe a religious work more beautiful and sincere, and although it is Buddhist, it is more Christian than all the works of our young Catholic writers, beginning with Claudel. People say it has a considerable success in Japan, and that is characteristic.

Dear Friend, how much I would like to come and see you in India! All the movements of my mind tend towards that direction. I fear I shall not be able to carry out this plan this winter. The two reasons which prevent me are my old father, 87-year old, whom one cannot well leave alone; and my own health, which has been rather affected after my voyage to England. My sister who will be my travelling companion and my interpreter cannot give an equal share of attention to my father and to myself; and we have no other near relatives left. But I hope for a voyage to Asia and a stay at Santiniketan. I have so much to learn from you! And I believe that I shall have there a mission to fulfil,—a predetermined duty till the end of my life. The union of Europe and Asia must be, in the centuries to come, the most noble task of mankind. As for myself, India from now on is not a foreign land, she is the greatest of all countries, the ancient country from which once I came. I find her again deep inside me.

Good bye, dear friend, forgive the length of this letter. I have been told that you have tired yourself very much during your tour across India. Take care of your health.

Believe in my deepest affection,

Written from Villeneuve (Vaud), Villa Olga, Switzerland.

To Ganesan

6 February, 1924

All joy at the news that the Mahatma is released! Joy to him, to Mahatma Gandhi and to all his people.

I hope he is not very seriously ill. Would that he knows that in Europe thousands of friends love him and thank him for the light that his life of sacrifice and of love is for them.

I am told that my little book on the Mahatma had appeared in Hindi and in Gujarati. Can you send me a specimen of these editions?

Please tell the Mahatma that W. W. Pearson who had a very devout love for him spent with me at Villeneuve an afternoon and another evening of last September two days before the fateful railway accident where he met with his death. In this last evening his thoughts were constantly about the Mahatma with a religious tenderness. Before his departure as if moved by a presentiment, he left with me the photograph which represents him with Andrews by the side of Gandhi in the Transvaal in 1913 or 1914. The photograph is here, near my table in my room in the Villa Olga.

Written from Villeneuve (Vaud), Villa Olga, Switzerland.

To Mahatma Gandhi

17 February, 1924

We join together to send you our message of love and admiration.

There you are, free again, after the glorious shade of the jail, in the sunshine of the battlefield.

May India be ready this time.

And may Europe also hear your voice in her wilderness?

Yours in the love of India and the service of Humanity,

This letter bore the joint signatures of Paul Richard and Romain Rolland and was addressed to Mahatma Gandhi, Sabarmati (India). It was written from Villeneuve, Switzerland.

To Mahadev Desai

24 February, 1924

. . . If I have unconsciously committed a few mistakes in the little book[1] that I have dedicated to him, let the Mahatma

[1]Romain Rolland's essay, first published in the review *Europe* subsequently published with modifications, by Stock (late 1923).

excuse me for the sake of the great love and veneration that
his life and philosophy have inspired in me. A European
may, often, be deceived in his judgment about an individual,
or a nation, of Asia. But his heart cannot be deceived, when
he finds in them the common God and universal love. As our
European Mahatma—Beethoven—sings in his *Ode to Joy*: Let
us—millions of human beings—embrace each other.

Yours,

This was written on a post-card depicting Lake Geneva, sent from
Villeneuve (Vaud), Switzerland.

To C. F. ANDREWS

28 October, 1924

Dear Friend,

I was expecting that you, or Nag, would accompany
Tagore during his journey to Europe and America. I was
disappointed at not seeing you,—all the more so, as in your
absence I could not be informed in time of Tagore's passage
and his duration of stay in Paris. So he left for America
without my having the chance of conversing with him. And
yet, I could have given him a lot of useful information for
this journey to a much varied land, divided into more than
twenty nations and innumerable enemy factions.

Your most interesting account of *A Day With Mahatma
Gandhi* is to appear in the November number of *La Revue
Européenne*, and I've told them to send you a few copies. The
Neue Zürcher Zeitung (the biggest German-language Swiss
newspaper) has also published it. I took the liberty of adding
a few introductory lines to the French version.

. . . Some Russian friends have written to tell me that the
Bolshevik government might be making some strange

advances to Gandhi. The Russian representative in Berlin, Mr Krestinsky, is supposed to have been instructed by the Russian Foreign Office to offer an official reception (?) to Gandhi and 'make use of the situation to spread activist (Bolshevik) propaganda among his adepts'. Furthermore, Krestinsky is said to have been asked to invite Gandhi to visit Russia. He has been authorized to give a subsidy towards publishing propaganda literature among the oppressed peoples of Asia, and he is to institute in the Oriental Club and Secretariat a scholarship bearing Gandhi's name for students who share his ideas (Gandhi's ideas, or Moscow's?). In conclusion, three Hindus are said to have been attached to him for this task: Manabendra Nath Roy, Bakandsha Rustem-Kala and Bairana Suviama. (I don't know the last two names, which are probably spelt wrong, but that of the Bolshevik Hindu Manabendra Nath Roy is enough to show the Marxist revolutionary character of the enterprise.) All this has been published in some Russian newspapers, such as *Rul* on 18 October.

I expect Gandhi will be shrewd enough to unravel Moscow's true motives, but I thought it was worth telling you about it, so that you can help to enlighten him if necessary. I admire the intelligence and energy of the Bolshevik government, but I am profoundy hostile to its ways of going about things which are totally lacking in frankness. Its policy in its struggle to destroy the present European system is to use all the great forces which are opposed to European imperialism, even those which are also opposed to the Bolshevik system of violence and oppression. The Soviet commissars and their propagandists pretend to adapt themselves to the ideas of the supporters of non-violence so as to make use of them; then, after compromising them, when they have no further use for them, they scornfully trample on them. They have many times tried to use the names of myself and Anatole France in this way, but for my part I have always energetically kept on my guard. I certainly prefer Moscow to Washington, and Russian Marxism to American and European imperialism. But I claim to be as independent of the one as I am of the other, 'above the battle'! The *Civitas Dei*, the holy city of non-violence and human fraternity must keep out of all alliances and compromises with the violent elements in any class or any party.

Very affectionately yours,

Written from Villeneuve (Vaud), Villa Olga, Switzerland.

To Rabindranath Tagore

27 March, 1925

My Very Dear Friend,

I have read with emotion the letter which you have taken the trouble to dictate to Kalidas Nag for me. I am deeply grateful to you for having done so at a time when you were still sore with the fatigue of travelling. I hope that rest in your own dear country, surrounded by faithful friends, has since restored to you that strength which is so precious to us.

As to reasons for your depression, they cannot be so soon removed. I quite understand it. I know how it must pain you to see your people carried away by violent political and social currents to which they abandon themselves blindly. Time and its fever, its narrow brutality, have effected a breach in the religious soul of ancient India. Her shortsighted desire aims at a goal which is too low and too near. It seems to have lost sight of her noble mission, her eternal aim. But this will last only for a while. And that which now is, no doubt, *had to be*: this is a common phenomenon in the universe. There is a Law hidden within this. It is for us to understand it, and without bending before its might (because our Law transcends it) to watch it take its course.

In every country of the world, men like us are alone. I

believe they have always been so. But considering that, in this our present age of paroxysms, all characters tend to become exaggerated and over-emphasized, the divergence appears wider between the crowd which exists from day to day, and the small number of men who keep in touch with the eternal; between the clamorous riot of people who, by means of murderous war and hate, seek to assert, one against the other, their 'Me' of the herd, their nations, and those who, having long passed that stage, seek to prepare the next, in order to receive therein the heirs to the present generation. The saying of Schiller, in *Don Carlos* which I have taken for a motto in my *Les précurseurs* is always true of us:

. . . *Iche lebe.*
Ein Burger derer, welche kommen werden.

'I am a fellow-citizen of those who will come later.'

Our home is the future. Indeed, even beyond the future, for we have built our nest in the tree of eternity; so we can defy the winds, and sing our melody serenely; like our blackbird-musicians of Europe who, installed at nightfall on high branches, sing their long fluty melopoeias for those who are at a distance. Like them who are in the light, whilst shadows already lengthen on the ground, it is for us to transmit our speck of light to the centuries to come.

But we also have the happiness of communicating it to each other. Throughout the world we are a small group inspired by the same ideas. And we should be stronger if we knew each other. For my part, I try to do so as much as I possibly can. And your brave journeys to the Far East and Far West have been undertaken with the same object. The second of these voyages has not been very successful. But the conditions prevailing were not favourable; and I don't think you should judge Ibero-Indian America by this annoying attempt. Of all these countries, Argentine is the most de-individualized. One ought to get into touch with the tragic soul (perhaps the most tragic of all our European races) of Mexico, of Indian Peru, and of Chile,—with that haughty

'Desolation', which is the title of a book of verses by one of
the noblest interpreters of that tragedy, Gabriela Mistral.*

I am addressing to Kalidas Nag, so that he may pass it on
to you, the manuscript of an article I am publishing in the
reviews of France and America for the eightieth birth-
anniversary (*post mortem*) of Carl Spitteler. I consider this Swiss-
German poet to be the greatest epic poet of Europe since
Goethe and Milton. I knew him during the war and I have
tried to express, in this article, the emotion and the joy which
I owe to his books. I have also asked them to send you at
Santiniketan the principal works of Spitteler—especially the
three great epic poems: the Olympian Spring, and the two
Prometheus. They have promised to do so. These works are
written in German, but I trust that amongst those who
surround you there will be found good translators, who will
read them to you or who will give you a résumé, as they are
of considerable dimensions. I warn you against the apprecia-
tions of German university men of letters. I can count only a
small number of those who really understand the exceptional
greatness of Spitteler; everything in him is far removed from
the official literary canons of modern Germany. He is (or
rather he was, for he died last December) a solitary giant in
the midst of European art. However, his solitude did not
weigh upon him. He was wise, brave and light-hearted. The
very inadequate pages which I have dedicated to him, will all
the same enable you to obtain a preliminary idea of the
character of his powerful work. Of all that Europe has
produced since several centuries, nothing seems to me so
much akin to the mythical and religious epics of India as these
poems. And, like the thinkers of India, he has a natural
genius for 'visualizing' thought; with him even abstractions
are plastic. I would request you, if you wish to gain a first
impression of his art, to read first, in 'Prometheus and

---

* 'Desolacion': by Gabriela Mistral (published in 1923); Editions
Nascimento, Santiago de Chile, Ahumada 272. Gabriela Mistral came to
Europe last summer, and I met her. She inspired me with a feeling of deep
respect.

Epimetheus', the admirable episode, Pandora. And then, if this gives you any pleasure, the song 'Die sieben schonen Amaschpand' and the song 'Apoll der Seher' in 'Olympischer Fruhling'.

How much obliged I am to Kalidas Nag for giving me your news! He is the most precious messenger we could have: the Indian Hermes, who goes from one to another, carrying the news of Asia to Europe, and of Europe to Asia, and joining their hands. But the poor boy is loaded with care and work; and it makes me sad to think that he has to struggle with so many troubles. I fear lest his health, which is not very strong should suffer for it. Your presence is his greatest happiness. He is the most loyal and most devoted of friends. My sister and I love him like a brother.

We shall not be in Switzerland during the month of June. We must take a trip to Germany, where great musical festivals invite us to Leipzig (several days of the Handel festival—those colossi of music, comparable to the massive blocks of the Alps)—then to Bonn and Cologne, where the great annual 'Rhenish Festival' takes place, the tradition of which had been interrupted by the war. These magnificent choral and instrumental *fêtes* are the most solid glory of Germany. They constitute for me a kind of religious office, the grand mass of the Soul of Europe. The Cantatas of J. S. Bach, the *Missa Solemnis* of Beethoven, the *Israel, Herakles* and *Samson* of Handel, are equal to the Bible,—and much nearer to us.

Au revoir, my very dear friend, whom we tenderly love. We send you our most fervent good wishes for your good health and peace of mind.

Your faithful,

I beg of you to excuse the insignificant pages which I have written as an introduction to *A Quatre Voix*. I did not want to do it, as they requested me to write them at the last moment, and I had not the time to treat such a great subject worthily. Moreover, I reserved for myself the task of doing so later on, after having permeated myself deeply with your works; and I still intend doing so. Be kind enough therefore not to attach any importance to this introduction, which is of no account to me.

I have just now received an excellent letter from André e Karpeles, who speaks of the melancholy pleasure she felt on seeing you in Italy. One would love to see the little group of friends reunited for once around you in India.

Written from Villeneuve (Vaud), Villa Olga, Switzerland.

To Santa Nag

1 May, 1925

My new Friend, Santa,

I send you my greetings of respect and affection, you with such a harmonious and beautiful name which evokes in me Italy as much as India (and even the flower of Ombria, Sanzio, Raffael of Urbi). I thank you for giving happiness to our dear Kalidas who deserves it so much. I am happy to know that you are together and I bless the road of life spreading itself before your feet. I do not ask that it should be easy, but may it be rich in mutual tenderness, and may it go up always towards the light and peace of the heart. 'Benedetta Santa'. It should be rather you who should bless us: because the gods listen more readily to youth and love.

Written from Villeneuve, Switzerland.

To Kalidas (and Santa) Nag

1 May, 1925

My Very Dear Friend,

How happy I am to learn that you have found the greatest of happiness,—the good and 'saintly' companion who will

share all your joys and sorrows and will mix her life with
yours in an identical river flowing towards the future. . .
And may the ray of the sun of love come to settle on you at a
time when your sky seems to be overcast with clouds of
worries. How beautiful and beneficial it is! May the little
fairy be blessed, who has dispelled the clouds and brought to
you the 'divine spark' from above (as Schiller sings, 'Joy,
daughter of Elysium')! And blessed is Tagore who, paternal-
ly, prepares this happiness for you!

My sister Madeleine also rejoices, with me. She sends her
kisses to Santa. And I embrace you.

Yours,

Written from Villeneuve, Switzerland.

To Emil Roniger

                                                    14 August, 1925
Dear Friend,

Rabindranath Tagore has written to us that his departure
has been postponed by a fortnight, on account of some
business. So it would be for tomorrow 15 August; and his
arrival in Europe would not take place until the first days of
September,—so he will be in Switzerland about the 7th. But
there can always be unforeseen obstacles at the last minute.
As long as our travellers have not left India, their plans can
still change.

I will try to prepare, between now and Tagore's arrival, a
draft of a programme-manifesto for the projected House of
Friendship. I shall submit it to you first.

Here is the role I would assign to the House of Friendship:

(1) *For the beginning*:

. . . Library, archives, information bureau:

a) to centralize names and addresses of those who, in all countries, will adhere to our programme of Europe-Asia intellectual union;

b) to collect, bit by bit, works published in any country, which can serve our objective. If the works themselves cannot be had, to collect a bibliography and any bibliographical information which can be of use to such of our adherents as may want to go deeply into a particular question (which, naturally, falls within the framework of our objective). For that, it will thus be necessary to have a correspondent in each country.

c) to set up a Club 'Eurasia' (a little on the model of the PEN Club founded by Galsworthy for all writers of the world,—but with a more clear-cut objective). The Club would meet once a year (which meeting, later, could be held sometimes in one country, sometimes in another);

d) to have a central Committee, with quite a limited number of members, but very representative of the major countries, which could be consulted on serious matters, on the doctrine to be instituted. Likewise, on directives to be given to publications. (For example, in the event of a war between Europe and Asia, what attitude to take? how to act?);

e) a Bulletin to be published quarterly, or at still longer intervals, (or which would appear on any important occasions), reporting the progress of the association, the main communications received, the decisions taken, if any. It would be concise and keep group members in touch with each other.

(2) *For later*:

a) to organize lectures and meetings, at the head office of the association,—then at other offices;

b) to set up abroad branches of the House of Friendship,—in Europe and in Asia;

c) to encourage works, theses, research,—and, if possible, give travel grants for studies on subjects,
assigned or approved, contributing to mutual understanding of the thought of Europe and Asia;
d) to centralize these works in a publishing house (and
in those allied to it, in foreign countries.

For the publishing house:

(1) The first preliminary question which must be settled
before undertaking any project: How many volumes per
year (on an average) will Rotapfelverlag publish?

After this number has been fixed, it will have to be
distributed in the first place *among the various projected series*
of publications. It has to be clearly seen in advance how
many volumes can be allocated under each group.
a) I do not know what are the various series which
Rotapfel may have started. The only important one,
which we have discussed, is the *Eurasia* Library,
within which can come the works of Gandhi, along
with the Asian works, Tagore, etc.
b) If Tolstoy were to be published as copiously as you
have indicated to me, he should, in that case, form a
group apart, by himself alone.
c) For pure European literature, there would be place
for few volumes per year. And thereby would be
eliminated the idea of publishing the complete works
of a single author: that would be an impossibility.
Frankly, one must resolve to select only the most
characteristic works.
d) But what should be the criterion for such selection?
In my opinion, we should eliminate works which are
of a *nationalistic* nature, or of *dilettante aestheticism*.
(Not that they cannot have their own interest, but
one must choose.) To be eliminated also are perhaps
works of art with too specialist a character, too
confined to coteries (like the poetry of Mallarmé). As

one must restrict oneself, one should take only works of a *universal* nature, those which are written for the whole of mankind, and the *constructive* (not negative, or sceptical) works, those that invigorate and unite.

e) It would be good to find, from each great country of Europe, works (poetry, novels, theatre) that are *characteristic* of the spirit of the race, containing whatever that race has as its best, productive, and *positive* (as opposed to *negative*).

f) To try to organize, in each country, a series of written studies on the essential values of that country (or of the races of a country), on what it brings as its own to the universal harmony of the human spirit.

g) To consider, later, the idea of a *bibliographical* magazine, with critical notices on the major works published in Europe and in Asia, during the quarter or the half-year.

Written from Villeneuve, Switzerland

To Mahatma Gandhi

1 October, 1925

My Dear Brother,

You will soon be receiving at Sabarmati Miss Madeleine Slade, whom you have been kind enough to admit to your Ashram. She is a dear friend of my sister and myself; I look upon her as a spiritual daughter and I am delighted that she is coming to put herself under your direction. I know how good it will be for her, and I am sure you will find in her one of your most staunch and faithful disciples. Her soul is full of admirable energy and ardent devotion; she is straightforward and upright. Europe cannot offer a nobler or more disin-

terested heart to your cause. May she bear with her the love
of thousands of Europeans, and my veneration.

Yours,

Written from Villeneuve, Switzerland.

To Kalidas Nag

26 November, 1925

My Dear Friend,

My sister who is in Paris for a few weeks and to whom I
sent on your last letter, tells me that you are waiting for my
authorization to publish my book on Mahatma Gandhi in
Bengali. I give it to you with great pleasure; I am merely
obliged to remind you that Ganesan has already brought out
other editions of my book in Hindi, Tamil and English.

I should like to reply to the various points you touch on in
your letter, but your letter is in English and my interpreter—
my sister—is away, so I don't know exactly what you say in
your letter, and I shall have to wait for my sister's return.
You see what comes of giving up writing in French in your
correspondence with me!

I have just written: 1) for a daily in the USA, a letter about
the wars of the Moroccan Riff and Syria, or more exactly on
the fatality of history which is governing European imperialism and leading to its ruin; 2) for a magazine of young Italians
oppressed by Fascism; another letter on the present duty of
free minds. After Madeleine returns, I will have her copy
these pages. And I'll send them on to you.

Don't be too harsh on Gandhi and his participation in
politics! The task is not the same for everyone, and there's
room in the Pantheon of great souls for both Tagore and
Gandhi; each of them saves an essential part of our human
heritage. If Gandhi succeeds in containing—or even merely

in delaying for twenty years—the violence which is building up and threatening to break its bounds, it will be a priceless benefit for India and the whole world, and that is worth the few apparent concessions to the world of politics which shock you! Beware lest, without him, the whole of the India you love should be inexorably submerged in the unleashed fury of political passions! By associating himself with politics, he moderates and humanizes them—I should rather say he 'divinizes' them, as the 'human' left to itself is not far from the animal! Nor should you forget the radiance he casts on many European minds whom he thus brings closer to Asia, and to whom India has become a holy land almost with the same status as Palestine. It is inevitable that much error should be mixed with much truth in these judgements, but this is the case with all new faiths. The spirit of humanity collaborates with the man of God to build the fruitful legend from which the new Gospel will spring.

I am writing to you in haste, as I have urgent work to do. I send you and our young sister Santa our most affectionate and friendly greetings.

Yours,

Written from Villeneuve, Switzerland.

To Madeleine Slade

17 December, 1925

My Dear Daughter,

How happy we have been with all your letters which tell us of your great joy, superior to your expectations,—joy to have found the Master of goodness, of love and of truth,—joy to have entered at last on the good and just way for which you have hunted so long, and where your energies will best deploy themselves.

You remember the word which embodies Wisdom in the third act of *Parsifal*: '*Dieuen*' (to serve). But in *Parsifal* it appears to be above all the mission of the woman. And it is—it ought to be—your lot. Every being conscious of his responsibilities feels himself joined to other beings, and endeavours to serve them with the best that is in him. Of all the paths of service that of the Mahatma is one of the straightest and most luminous. It leads to the peace of the soul. May you taste of it! When you have gathered it distribute to us a few pieces of the delicious fruit!

Do not forget the light of Europe upon the roads of Asia! Make those around you enjoy it! Take and give!—I can see you out there in the morning before dawn on the nocturnal roads around Sabarmati, by the side of the Mahatma, singing to yourself the divine melody of the Hymn of Joy. There, it would not be out of its element.

I do not know how to thank you enough for the trouble that you took in noting down for us in detail all the days of your voyage. To us they are—and will remain—a unique testimony of your March to the Star—of this new pilgrimage of the Shepherds, who go towards the torch of the Orient.

We are keeping fairly well,—kept up by incessant occupation and the passion of work, which is as necessary to me as the air which I breathe. Long since I should have fallen by the way if the creative fire and the mission of work had not carried me on!

Tell the Mahatma how much I thank him for the letter which he has written me, in spite of his immense activity—and how much I rejoice to know of his being near to you, and of your being near to him! In this old Europe so full of genius, but at the moment covered as it were with a cloud in my beloved land of France, where still there blossom so many souls, simple and pure, courageous and charming, but who live apart leaving the government of the world and the guidance of opinion to the worst,—I fight, alone, without the hope of saving those who do not wish to be saved. But I sow for the future the corn that will (ripen) when we shall be

1 Romain Rolland (second from right) with Tagore (on his left) at Villeneuve, 26 June 1926. (*Rod Schlemmer*)

no more. The grain does not come from me: I have searched it out through all the world. The most beautiful is that which my bird Spirit has brought back from the Orient,—the grain of the Great Soul, which itself has gathered grain from the Sacred Books of Asia (and we have recognized there, mixed with Hinduism, the savour of the Gospel. All the seeds of life come from the same divine granary.) We are a handful of religious souls in Europe who thank the Mahatma for rendering to us the good pure corn separated from the tares.

My daughter, it will now be for you to bless us. You are giving of yourself for us, and you are at the source of benedictions.

Will you ask once of your great friend and Master, to offer up with you a brief and silent prayer for us, for our peace, for the salvation of ours, so that we may know to the last how to be vanquished without bending.

Mira, I embrace you. A happy Christmas and New Year from the lands of snow and the cradle of the Epiphany.

Your friend,

To Rabindranath Tagore

22 December, 1925

Dear Friend,

Often I think of you. The lofty melancholy of the last letter which you wrote to me often haunts me. My mind crosses the seas, and I come into the room where the faithful Nag listens with sacred attention to your meditation. I am seated in a corner, not far from you, and I also am listening.

What a contrast between the immense human society that has been formed in the world round your name, between the resonances which vibrate in thousands of human hearts in all countries and the moral solitude which surrounds you in your own country!

This is undoubtedly the fate of those who speak to the universe, of those who do not shut themselves up within the bounds of the enclosure (of the small country). You are too vast for it. Your very presence troubles the dwellers of this enclosure. Who knows it better than I, an old Frenchman, held in my own country as a stranger! My little province of Nivernais will live in future in my *Colas Breugnon*. And she has not even read it. For having defended during the war the highest soul of France, her genius for humanity, France denies me; the *Théâtre français* has just declared that they would never stage a work of the man who had written '*Au-dessus de la Mêlée*'. Such is the law, ironical and tragic. He who wishes to save his people is an enemy of the people, as is said in the beautiful play by Ibsen.

I think that we, the men 'above the battles', we are the greatest fighters, the eternal fighters. Our war knows no compromise, no truce, no treaty! It has no other victory, no other peace to expect save inward victory and peace. But we have to conquer and maintain them against all blows of destiny. Our universe is within us. It is for us to discover its laws of divine harmony.

For a long time you possess its mastery. It is the secret of your power over our hearts that we hear resounding under your fingers this 'music of the spheres' which fills your room. I listen to it (with Nag).

The western year is going out. It is going away in the whirling fury of wild hot winds, which for the last two or three days are moving about howling in the mountain ranges and have suddenly made the gathered snows melt. The 'Foehn' as it is called here. How easy it is to understand that the ancients had personified the winds! I heard them tonight, shrieking, laughing, howling like a pack of unchained spirits—or like the whirling shades in Dante's Hell!

But opposite my window my ancient walnut, century-old, denuded of leaves, stands passive with its great body, heroic and naked; and the ends of the branches hardly bow at the passing of the storm.

Dear friend, I send you the affectionate wishes of your friends of the West! May the thought of their love be to you an additional source of strength!

I hope that the coming year will not pass without our seeing each other, and I beg you to believe me with all my heart your friend who admires you and who loves you.

Written from Villeneuve, Switzerland.

TO JAWAHARLAL NEHRU

11 May, 1926

Dear Mr Jawaharlal Nehru,

I was happy to receive your letter and that of our saintly friend Gandhi. Your name was known to us. Just within the last few days, we read it in a speech published by the *Hindustan Times*.

My sister and I will be very pleased to see you. Will it be possible, for you and Madame Nehru, to come over here, one afternoon next week when it is fine, to have tea and to spend a few hours at the Villa Olga? Do please tell me which day will suit you best between Wednesday the 19th and Saturday the 22nd May. Should the weather be bad on the day you choose, you have only to send a telegram in the morning, saying that you are postponing your visit to another day.

I hope that Madame Nehru will soon feel the good effects of the Swiss climate.

Is it not your little daughter, who is in the International School at Geneva? Her teacher, Miss Hartoch, is an excellent friend of ours. She is the best and the most devoted woman. You can be sure that your little daughter could not be in wiser and more affectionate hands.

Please accept, dear Mr Nehru, my friendly affection.

The Villa Olga is near (a little above) the Hotel Byron. If you come by boat, it is ten minutes from the landing place of Villeneuve. If you come by rail, you can get down at Territet Station, take the Vevey-Villeneuve electric tram (for Villeneuve), which passes in front of the station, and get down at the Hotel Byron Stop.

Written from Villeneuve (Vaud), Villa Olga, Switzerland.

TO RABINDRANATH TAGORE

8 July, 1926

Dear Great Friend,

You are always with us. Although every day of your tour takes you further away from us, we preserve here the warmth of your presence, the affectionate light of your eyes, and of your dear talks. Accept my loving thanks for these twelve beautiful days which you have granted us. They are now part of the most precious treasure of our life.

I would have liked to show you my affection better. Not to be able to speak to you directly in your language was a discomfort. However faithfully and discreetly my sister Madeleine translated our words, they could not have the intimacy of a tête-à-tête. This problem of the need of a common language dominates all our efforts at universal *rapprochement*. I continue talking with you, in silence. I follow you on your long pilgrimage in search of fraternal minds. The best are often those most difficult to reach, those who remain aloof, silent, concentrated. Your plan to come back another year, and to settle down for some months in one country is the best, I believe, to make all these affluents come to you.

Never forget the magic power of your name and all it represents for an élite of Europe! Undoubtedly it knows you only partially, by imperfect translations. (Who indeed knows you, even among those who are nearest to you?) But Duhamel has just told me these last days that there is something more essential than the direct effect of books—it is their 'fragrance'—these mysterious emanations of a God-pervaded soul. There exist a multitude of poets whom one reads and whose art is admired. But very few radiate this enchantment which awakens and exalts the forces of life. You are one of these good genii. May you still for a long time to come help and guide the free pilgrime on the arduous road of justice and truth—or, as said the Greeks, of the beautiful and the true.

Take care of yourself. We fear the winter in America for you. We send you and all those who are with you, your son, Mr and Mrs Mahalanobis, our cordial friendship. To you our gratitude and deep affection.

Yours,

I have written to Salvemini and to President Masaryk. I shall soon write to Mr Mahalanobis.

Written from Villeneuve (Vaud), Villa Olga, Switzerland.

To Madeleine Slade

26 September, 1926

Dear Friend,

I find, at last, an hour for conversing with you, and, through you, with your Bapu.

I am replying to your letter of the end of July, and I return to my replying that Gandhi could not take part in the conference for Christian Young Men at Helsingfors. Those regrets are accentuated since my meeting with several of these young men and with K. T. Pual.

The question is in no way, as you think, one of fashionable enthusiasm for Gandhi's person, or a superficial infatuation for the doctrine of Gandhi. No, there is not even a question of it,—the fact more unexpected, but indisputable, is that the person, the action, the life and the faith of Gandhi have been the strongest stimulant for European Christianity. Neither you nor Gandhi could have expected it, and it was scarcely the goal for which the Mahatma was searching. But great actions have unexpected repercussions; and often their effect equals or surpasses in importance the effect which had been expected and wished by the man of God. Because, after all, it is not he who acts; it is, by means, God.

The fact is then that Young Christian Europe has seen in Gandhi the purest Christian (without knowing it) of today,—the man who, over and above all the priests and pastors, resumes the direct tradition with the spirit of the Gospel.

That he has found himself in possession of immense influence over these young Christians, for interpreting to them their own doctrine, and for showing them the path in an hour of agonizing uncertainties and doubts.

Once more, it may be, that Gandhi did not wish this. But once more, another greater than he willed it for him. And he has not the right to escape from it in the future. Because, however imperious may be his Indian task, the human task envelops it and surpasses it. And whatever may be his personal faith in Hinduism,—the most ardent fire, the most divine of all faith, the eternal is that which feels in common with all, and not which differentiated. God is in the centre of the Bush. And he who hears Him speak, and repeats what He says, speaks for all.

Now, the Christianity of today is consumed by the anguish of a problem of conscience and faith that not one of the chiefs or official representatives has the power to solve. I find acute expressions of this in the works of a professor of the University of Rome which I have just received: *Ubi Christianus?* and *Dottrina di Cristo,* by Luigi Trafelli. The author, who is undoubtedly a tortured conscience, starts with the declaration that the 'Metanoia' or 'evangelical conversion' where the preaching of Jesus begins, is an absolute overthrow and the complete transformation of the values, which, in the normal life of men, are the most appreciated. It is necessary to strip 'the old man' and to redress 'the new man', who will not be able to enter into the Kingdom of God, if he does not sacrifice all half-duties to the whole duty, and all compromises of the world to the will of perfection. 'Be thou then perfect as is thy Father in Heaven'. No concessions to the world: 'Leave all and follow Me'.

Now, after having examined the perpetual conflicts of this order with the worldly order, and all the 'combinations' imagined by the Church and the pseudo-believers, for reconciling them, Luigi Trafelli asks himself the mournful question: 'Do Christians still exist?' and concludes: 'No, they exist no more',—and he admits himself: 'I am not a Christian.'—but adds: 'At least, I have not got the hypocrisy to call myself Christian, as do the churches, while betraying the express word of Christ'.

They question is made particularly tragic owing to the social crisis which is passing over Europe, the world (and especially the country which is the seat of official catholicism, Italy).

At the present hour, the power of the State in Italy has reached a sovereignty which is veritably demoniac. Everything is sacrificed to it, religious conscience is trampled under its feet. The individual soul is annihilated. He who resists the 'Public Will' (translated by one or two leaders who incarnate it) is, or will be, crushed. A Mussolini with formidable cynicism displays this docrine, accepted by millions of Italians, which will certainly spread before long in Europe and America, (above all in America).

Now, what are the guides of religious conscience doing at this hour? They dare not take the responsibility of the nameless sufferings into which they would throw those who ask their advice, by saying to them,—'Resist! Be

persecuted!'—the worst, the most mediocre, think of their
tranquillity. The best remind themselves of old Tolstoy who
was in despair at seeing his disciples persecuted while he
could not succeed in getting persecuted himself: because
power is too cunning not to treat with care the men who are
in broad daylight, and severely the obscure. The result is that
all search for, and teach, compromises—the inner lie; and the
soul degrades itself.

The young men realize this, they listen for the voice of the
Gospel which will say to them: 'The Duty is there'. The
voice speaks not. They are left. It is for this reason that so
many young Christians look towards Gandhi.

. . . You say to me, my friend, that it is for me to reply to
them. . . . No. I cannot. It is necessary to see me as I am, and
not lend to me a faith, thoughts, a mission that I have not
got.

I am not a Christian. I am not a Gandhist, I am not a
believer in a revealed religion. I am a man of the Occident
who, in all love and in all sincerity, searches for the truth.
That which I strive to teach to myself is for others, it is never
to believe one's own thoughts, never to say that one knows
that which one only 'believes' or hopes, to say exactly that
which one knows,—nothing more,—and, be it that one
understands or does not understand, to conserve intact
energy and love. The word of the introduction to *The Life of
Michel Angelo*: 'See men and life as they are,—and as they are,
love them and act. That is my role. And it is also to discover
and make known to others all the sources of strength, all the
hearths of light, which exist in the world. The heroes and the
saints. I say: "Take, and drink"!'

But my role is not to speak in the name of a religion which
I have not. Let those speak who have!

. . . We have lately had a visit from a gay American who is
making an express tour of all the celebrated men of the globe;
five minutes for each one. His name is Buchanan, and he has
seen Gandhi at the beginning of the year. He says that Gandhi
said, regarding my book on him—'It is literature' ('*C'est de la*

litterature')—No, it is not altogether just. It should be said: 'It is love' ('*C'est de l'amour*'). Everybody knows that love does not see very exactly. My book must often be erroneous. How could it be otherwise? I knew nothing of the atmosphere of India, or of the language. I made the *tour de force* in six to twelve months, from imagination, after the books I had read, all a great life, and that of a people who were far away and unknown to me. It was very audacious! But love did not give me the liberty not to imagine, and—that which I loved, my joy, my enthusiasm,—not to share them with my brothers of Europe. In that, I believe I have succeeded. If I have sometimes, often, mispresented the character and the thought of Gandhi, may he pardon me!—I have often asked myself what Christ would have thought of the narratives of his disciples!—In any case, true or false, I have not written for 'literature'. (The litterateurs scarcely consider me as one of them). I wrote to relieve my heart.

. . . We are pretty well, in spite of the fact that I have just been laid up for a fortnight with intestinal fever. Madeleine has spent a little time in Savoie and we have had beautiful walks together. Since August the splendour of the summer has been marvellous.

I am not surprised that you feel yourself 'at home' in India. Did not you tell us that you have gypsy blood? And you have seen that, according to the latest discoveries the gypsies unquestionably had India for their cradle. You return to your point of departure.

Madeleine and I send you our most affectionate thoughts. To Bapu my filial respect,—in spite of the fact that I am corporally older than him. But the soul belongs to other cycles of time than the body.

Your,

Written from Villeneuve (Vaud), Villa Olga, Switzerland.

To Gabriel Monod-Herzen

7 October, 1926

My Very Dear Gabriel,

Each one of your visits makes us feel an increasing affection for you. Be sure that your life is greatly valuable— and not only for us—for the friends to come, for the future. You have before you a magnificent task, which you are worthy of. You will be the civil engineer who will open the road between the mind of Europe and that of Asia. Your multiple knowledge, both scientific and religious, as also your talents have marked you for it in advance.

But this precious life of yours, which is in your hands, needs to be looked after. It is fragile. During the years to come, it will be necessary for you to exercise a discipline to ensure the soundness of its health. Forge your armour! Don't leave for India without testing beforehand all the components of the breast-plate. If need be, I would even like you to move away from Paris a year before your departure and retire to a place in the open air where you would invigorate both your body and mind. You would carry to this healthy retreat the materials for your thesis which you would complete later in Asia, on the spot. Remember our talk with Mukerji! I imagine for you, particularly, a major work on the great Precursors of Europe and Asia who were the first to conceive, desire and attempt the *rapprochement*, the union and the bringing together of the Spirit of the two halves of the old continent. I would call it 'The Arches'. It's a beautiful name.

I am only one of the piers, lying in ruins. But in an etching by Piranesi, with grass, bushes and goats grazing on it, it doesn't look that bad!

Mukerji is in Paris (41 boul. Haussmann). He has written to me an overflowing letter. I have given him your address. If you happen to see him, do remind him to send me the documents he was kind enough to mention to me.

Please do kiss Edouard and Claudia for me on both cheeks. . .

With greetings paternal, fraternal,

Written from Villeneuve, Switzerland.

To Rabindranath Tagore

11 November, 1926

Dear Friend,

Whom I revere and whom I love, I would like these words to reach you at Balatonfured, before you take again the road to the East, and to ring you our salutation, our *Au revoir* and our affectionate wishes, mine and those of Europe which you have honoured by this noble visit—from the North to the South, from the Occident to the Levant—despite the great hardships and the danger for your health.

We understand only too well that you should not expose yourself to the risk of a second crossing of Europe in order to come back to Switzerland and to France. But we deeply regret, my sister and I, not to see you once again. One must learn to limit oneself! You have given us much.

What I most regret is that circumstances have forced us to devote a large part of our conversations to discussing contemporary and depressing subjects—that unfortunate Italy—instead of devoting ourselves, as we would both have liked, to things eternal. Be assured that they occupy my mind very much—more indeed than the ephemeral vicissitudes of the eternal *mêlée*. And I would have liked to exchange with you—but all alone (with my good and dear interpreter, my sister)—our thoughts concerning the soul and destinies, the invisible, the omnipresent and the essence eternal. These beautiful days, at the end of autumn, with the golden sun on multicoloured forests, like a tapestry of Flanders, would have favoured these meditations by ourselves and in subdued tones. But one must be contented with having them from afar, in thought, from soul to soul. Mine will follow you all along your return voyage.

In the next two years, Europe will celebrate the centenary of two of her greatest sons (the third, of Goethe, will follow in a few years):—on 26 March 1927, the centenary of Beethoven's death; in August 1928, that of Tolstoy's birth. My health permitting, I shall try to take part in the two principal festivals of commemoration: for Beethoven in Vienna;—for Tolstoy in Moscow. I would have liked to meet you there too. Ordinarily I do not participate in any of these commemorations, for I think that the best way of celebrating the great dead is to live and to act according to their example and to walk on the path they have traced. But I make an exception for Beethoven and Tolstoy (and I add Goethe). I am the child of their thought, of their sufferings, of their battles. And I must bring them the testimony of my love and of my faith.

During these last few weeks (22 October 1926) I have acquired a letter by Goethe, written on the 22 October, 1826 (exactly a century ago), where he speaks of India with Wilhelm von Humboldt. One senses in it the attraction and the fear which the world of Indian thought and art caused within him. He seems to be afraid of losing the severe equilibrium which all through his life he had imposed upon his tormented life. (For the true Goethe is so little known! And his 'olympian' peace is but the result of his will ever awake after a life-long battle against his 'demon'.) In this same letter he speaks of his second *Faust*, of the magnificent '*Helena*' episode which he was going to publish. It would have given me pleasure to show it to you.

Goodbye, dear and beloved friend. May a friendly fate enfold you within its wings! My sister sends you her very affectionate thoughts. You are always, in spirit, with us. Remember us to the friendly memory of your children and of your companions, and pray believe me.

Your faithful friend,

Confidential: I know not whether you have read in the papers of the terrible scenes which happened in Italy during the last fifteen days, since the outrage and bestial massacre of this 15-year-old child at Bologna. Almost throughout the whole of Italy frightful scenes of violence, robberies and destruction; more than five to six thousand innocent people wounded. I learn this morning that at Naples the house of Benedetto Croce had been invaded, as well as the house of the well-known dramatist Roberto Bracco. A gifted draughtsman whom I knew, Scalarini, is dying.

The affair of Colonel Ricciotti Garibaldi, arrested in France as an *agent-provocateur* of Fascism for fomenting false plots against Mussolini and receiving money from Mussolini's chiefs of police, in order to hand over the anti-fascist refugees in France and to compromise her hospitality in the eyes of the world, throws a sinister light upon this political system of crime and hypocrisy.

Often I have accused myself for having disturbed your rest when I took away from you the confidence you had in your Italian hosts. However, I had no other interest in my mind but your glory, which I value more than your rest. I did not want devils misusing your sacred name in the annals of history. Forgive me if my intervention has caused you some restless hours. The future (the present already) will show you that I have acted as your faithful and vigilant guide.

Written from Villeneuve (Vaud), Villa Olga, Switzerland.

TO MAHATMA GANDHI

14 November, 1926

My Dear Friend,

I have received your letter sent to me by Mira, and I thank you for it most affectionately. But I don't understand at all what 'the Poet' could have said to you. I have never said or written anything to Tagore about the lines from your pen published in the *Liber Amicorum*. I didn't discuss them with anyone in the Poet's entourage, and if I had, it would only have been to express the joy they gave me and the gratitude I felt for them. How could I possibly have thought of complaining of a judgment like yours? I regard it as one of the honours of my life to have been able to put my efforts to your service and to spread your thought in the world. I am proud of my role as 'free servant', far from protesting against it! It grieves me to see such thoughts attributed to me.

I can't explain it at all; it must be one of the those trivial pieces of hearsay which are born for no good reason, grow as they circulate and cause so many misunderstandings. This one must be entirely effaced, as it is quite baseless.

My dear friend, I love and venerate you. Be what you have always been, both to me and to others, to the end of your life: a totally straightforward and sincere man, not seeking to please or to make compliments and not saying a word more than he thinks! All self-interest fades in your presence, for you set the example, and the writer that I am yields to the man of action that you are.

Please believe in my profound respect and faithful affection.

Written from Villeneuve (Vaud), Villa Olga, Switzerland.

To Kalidas Nag

6 December, 1926

My Dear Friend,

It will be a hundred years ago, next 26 March, that Beethoven, the hero of music, died in Vienna. The whole world is going to celebrate the event. Solemn commemorations have been announced in all countries, and even the enemy States are going to participate.

I thought India could associate itself with it through the publication of some words or messages in its big magazines, and that it would not be without interest to recall that

Beethoven had been attracted by Indian thought. Here are
some documents which you may find useful. They are copies
I have made of Beethoven's manuscripts. Beethoven had
himself copied these passages from translations (published,
or unpublished) of Indian poetry, no doubt much adapted to
the European spirit. The exact sources of them have not been
traced, except for the fragment III: 'Aus Gott floss alles', said
to be taken from the fourth and fifth acts of *Sakuntala*, in
Forster's translation. The hymn number eleven appears to be
the same as a hymn in Sanskrit translated into English by H.
Th. Colebroocke.

May I add these biographical details:

In 1808 Hammer-Purgstall, the renowned Austrian orien-
talist, returned to Vienna from Asia. Thanks to the friendship
of Count Rjewusky, he founded a periodical publication for
making oriental literature better known in Europe; this was
the *Fundgruben des Orients*, the first number of which
appeared on 6 January 1809.

Beethoven, who happened to be then in Vienna, at the
height of his genius and glory (in those years he was writing
the symphony in C minor and the *Pastoral*), entered into
relations with him. Two letters, which have been preserved,
show that Hammer-Purgstall, who admired him, had
'communicated to him unknown treasures in the form of a
manuscript', for which Beethoven thanked him profusely.
Furthermore, Hammer had written for Beethoven a poem of
an Indian opera, which Beethoven called 'herrliches'; and the
great musician looked forward to discussing it with Hammer
while at the same time learning more about Indian music.
But he was ill then. The project was deferred and later on,
other circumstances went against its execution. Only, among
the papers of Hammer there has been found a '*Memnons
Dreiklang*, nachgeklungen in Dewajani, einem indischen
Schäferspiele', (an Indian pastoral) which was no doubt the
poem intended for Beethoven.

But what attracted Beethoven even more than the poetry
of India was its religious thought; his letters and notes from

1809 to 1816 contain signs of his painstaking readings of translations done by Hammer. The enclosed pieces are some such examples which have been preserved.

It is important to note this awakening of a passionate curiosity and attraction of the European mind towards the thought of Asia which, some years later, in 1819, found expression in the publication of Goethe's poetical masterpiece *Westöstlicher Divan* (Beethoven fell in love with it), and in the formation of the personality of Schopenhauer.

I am leaving these fragments of Beethoven for you to read in German, hoping that you will not find it difficult to have them translated. Their value lies less in what they say than in the indication they give of the orientation of Beethoven's mind, in its maturity, towards the thought of Asia.

These facts are known to German musicographers who have made a special study of Beethoven. But they are not known to the public at large. I think India will be happy to know them.

★ ★ ★ ★ ★

This much for today. My sister Madeleine is in Paris, for two or three weeks, and I am overloaded with work.

I am having other documents sent to you, which are of a greatly different nature: a follow-up of enquiries on the abominable crimes and violence let loose in Italy during these last few months; and a book (which Henri Barbusse, will send you on my request), *Les Bourreaux*, relating the inquiry he conducted personally in Romania and Bulgaria, which are now exposed to a monstrous White Terror. You must have these documents. India seems to me to be duped by Fascist propaganda, signs of which I notice, with regret, even in the magazine of your dear father-in-law whom I respect and love. And our great Tagore, after his visit to Mussolini, has once again been ill advised to have himself received and patronized by the criminals who are torturing Bulgaria and Romania. It is no use telling him that now, it is too late. And moreover, I have the impression that if anything to that effect is said to him, it would only pain him, without convincing him. But his guides and advisers are much to blame. With the best of intentions (no one doubt that), they have, during this journey to Europe, shown themselves to be of an extreme frivolity. They have seen only the outer aspect, the lecture-going public, the social functions. They have not tried to penetrate, behind the official or officious façade, into the freedom-loving and oppressed conscience of Europe, which has been disappointed and, I am afraid, alienated by their tourist-like attitudes. I am doing my best to lessen these misunderstandings among my friends of Europe. I know only too well how dangerous a ground today's blood-stained Europe is for a foreigner who, without precautions, ventures into it as an observer. Perhaps India would be as dangerous a country for me if I went there. But that is why I am not going there, so as not to find myself involved in existing dissensions between parties of great men like Tagore and Gandhi, not to speak of the deeper chasm lying between Indians and Englishmen (but there, it would not be difficult for me to take sides: my choice is made:—For you).

Good bye, my very dear friend. May this letter bring to you, to Madame Santa and to your little darling my European Christmas greetings and my best wishes for your health and happiness.

Yours,

Written from Villeneuve (Vaud), Villa Olga, Switzerland.

To H. Marichi

15 January, 1927

My cordial thanks. . . But let me tell you how shocked I have been to see in this number, next to the sacred faces of

Gandhi and Tagore, the face of the worst of tyrants: Mussolini. You don't know the horro it rouses among the free souls of Europe. If in India there are men who adore brute force which crushes justice and liberty, let them prostrate themselves before the new idol who is coming to them from Italy! But let them not commit the impropriety of carrying that bloody idol to the sanctuaries of Santiniketan and Sabarmati! . . .

To D. B. KALELKAR

17 March, 1927

. . . National pride, in Europe, against which I have spent my life fighting, is such a terrible scourge that I see its shadow everywhere and wherever I see it showing itself I am on my guard. True, the situation is not at all the same in India and in Europe, but I know only too well with what rapidity this moral epidemic can spread, so that passing from a legitimate awareness of one's personality, of one's duties and legitimate rights it becomes a morbid hypertrophy of 'I'—national or racial—trampling underfoot everyone else. Today it is a permanent danger to humanity. Watching it calls for the severe control and firm hand of great directors of the conscience of peoples, such as our master Gandhi and yourself. And since neither he nor you will be there for ever, you must train for the role of pilots those who will, after you are gone, command the ship. We are in the fierce tempest of the world. The helmsman cannot close his eyes even for a second. In your letter there is a profound thought which has become engraved in my memory.

'In fact no knowledge can ever be foreign. It is a thing of the Spirit.'

This utterance makes us brothers—sons of the same father.

All the differences of opinion between us are secondary. . .

Written from Villeneuve (Vaud), Villa Olga, Switzerland.

To Bruno Scanferla

7 September, 1927

Dear Bruno Scanferla,

I clasp your hands cordially. Thank you for your letter.

The outer spectacle of the world and its convulsions is only a veil covering the profound and powerful eternal Life, the inner Ocean. It is not at all bad that the men of Europe, attracted naturally by action and, most often, carried along from birth to death by the whirlwind of tumultuous semblances, find themselves at this moment pushed back from this maelstrom as much by its brutality as by their own disgust. Thus are they perforce brought back to the inner life, which is the true life, and the source of which was in danger of drying up in Europe. One must learn again that self-concentration which opens up the gates of that limitless Being, whom each of us holds within him, without realizing it. It is an immense wealth which, sooner or later, will reveal itself before their eyes, when they have learnt again to see in this full light.

Lately, I have had long conversations with the greatly talented physicist and biologist of India, Sir Jagadis Chunder Bose, the one who, after thirty years of strict scientific observations and thanks to the invention of marvellous precision instruments, has succeeded in measuring and recording the living sensitiveness of plants (and even of the minerals), and thus, in demonstrating, through these achievements, the unity of universal life. His method blends the severest observation and experimentation of western

science with the Asian faculties of concentration, which
finally achieves identity at the depths of that universal Being
whom everyone carries in him, with the living object
observed. He says: 'When I study a tree, a plant, while
observing them in a rigorously objective manner (or better,
while letting them trace, by themselves, the graphs of their
reactions through the recording instruments invented by
me), I *am* the tree or the plant, and I myself become their
recording instrument.'

We possess the key for seeing living beings, and if we can
manage to handle it well, we shall be free from our isolation
and from all our oppressing doubts. But such a state can be
obtained only through a long discipline of mind. It is good
that it should be a great scientist, used to rigorous methods,
who comes to remind us of that. Our intuition of the heart,
the revelations of art, they have already made us feel it. Now
science brings us its confirmation.

Cordially yours,

If you read English, I recommend these two books to you:
1) Sir Jagadis Chunder Bose: *Plant Autographs and their Revelations*
(1927); 2) Patrick Geddes: *The Life and Work of Sir Jagadis C. Bose*
(Longmans, Green & Co., London, 1920).

To Swami Shivananda

12 September, 1927

Dear and Respected Swami Shivananda,

Allow a Frenchman who profoundly admires Sri Ramakrishna, to address himself to you who had the good fortune to
be his personal disciple.

A year ago, my sister, Madeleine Rolland, and myself read the
Life of Sri Ramakrishna and other publications which have

been dedicated to him by the Advaita Ashrama. I want to make known in the West that divine source of love and light. Nothing is more necessary to the humanity of our time than this revelation of the harmonious unity of all religious faiths, than this communion with God, manifold in form and yet Himself without form, who is the Being of all living beings.

But it is an extremely delicate task to translate (that is to say, to transpose) into a western book a personality so fundamentally Indian as that of Sri Ramakrishna. For, some of his religious experiences would be incomprehensible to almost the entire European public, and will even run the risk of concealing the most essential qualities of his life and thought, which could be of powerful assistance to it. That is why I am proceeding slowly; I am waiting until there appears in myself a living and true harmony of the work which I wish to write.

It is very precious to me to be able to communicate directly with you who saw with your own eyes this extraordinary man. Our epoch, too intellectualistic as it is, has a tendency to doubt the human existence of all the superhuman personalities of history. Even when it pretends to respect the lofty ideals, of which they were the torches, it sees in them only symbols created by the spirit of a race and of an age; one sees today those who deny that Jesus or Buddha had ever existed. It will not be slow in doing the same for Sri Ramakrishna, if his living witnesses do not leave in writing the proof of his life amongst them on earth. I should like to make known to the European public your direct testimony.

I wish also to ask you some enlightenment on an important question: the problem of suffering with Ramakrishna. I have read lately an excellent article in *Prabuddha Bharata* on the question of 'service' with Vivekananda and Ramakrishna, in which it was maintained that the great disciple had only drawn out the consequences of his Master's teachings,—of his 'adoration of the Divine in men', and that there was no disagreement between them. But it appears to me that the most essential feature of the personality of Vivekananda was

the mournful and heroic obsession of universal suffering and
of evil: to fight against or to console. Is it not the same central
idea, quite different from the universal Divine Vision, which
filled Ramakrishna with ecstasy of joy and with great faith in
the Eternal? What was his attitude with regard to the cruel
injustices of Nature and of society, of unfortunate people, and
of those who are oppressed or persecuted? Was he content
simply to love them? Did he not seek to help them? And has
he not precisely destined his great disciple Vivekananda to
that work?

Believe me, dear Swami Shivananda.

Yours affectionately,

To Sigmund Freud

5 December, 1927

Dear and Respected Friend,

I thank you for being so kind as to send me your lucid and
spirited little book. With a calm good sense, and in a
moderate tone, it pulls off the blindfolding bandage of the
eternal adolescents, which we all are, whose amphibian spirit
floats between the illusion of yesterday and. . .the illusion of
tomorrow.

Your analysis of religions is a just one. But I would have
liked to see you doing an analysis of *spontaneous religious
sentiment* or, more exactly, of religious *feeling*, which is
wholly different from *religions* in the strict sense of the word,
and much more durable.

What I mean is: totally independent of all dogma, all credo,
all Church organization, all Sacred Books, all hope in a
personal survival, etc., the simple and direct fact of *the feeling
of the 'eternal'* (which can very well not be eternal, but simply
without perceptible limits, and like oceanic, as it were).

This sensation, admittedly, is of a subjective character. But as it is common to thousands (millions) of men actually existing, with its thousands (millions) of individual nuances, it is possible to subject it to analysis, with an approximate exactitude.

I think you will class it also under the *Zwangsnurosen*. But I have often had occasion to observe its rich and beneficent power, be it among the religious souls of the West, Christians or non-Christians, or among those great minds of Asia who have become familiar to me and some of whom I count as friends. Of these latter, I am going to study, in a future book, two personalities who were almost our contemporaries (the first one belonged to the late 19th century, the second died in the early years of the 20th) and who revealed an aptitude for thought and action which proved strongly regenerating for their country and for the world.

I myself am familiar with this sensation. All through my life, it has never failed me; and I have always found in it a source of vital renewal. In that sense, I can say that I am profoundly 'religious'—without this constant state (like a sheet of water which I feel flushing under the bark) affecting in any way my critical faculties and my freedom to exercise them—even if that goes against the immediacy of the interior experience. In this way, without discomfort or contradiction, I can lead a 'religious' life (in the sense of that prolonged feeling) and a life of critical reason (which is without illusion). . .

I may add that this 'oceanic' sentiment has nothing to do with my personal yearnings. Personally, I yearn for eternal rest; survival has no attraction for me at all. But the sentiment I experience is imposed on me as a fact. It is a *contact*. And as I have recognized it to be identical (with multiple nuances) in a large number of living souls, it has helped me to understand that that was the true subterranean source of *religious energy* which, subsequently, has been collected, canalized and *dried up by the Churches*, to the extent that one could say that it is inside the Churches (whichever they may be) that true 'religious' sentiment is least available.

What eternal confusion is caused by words, of which the same one here sometimes means: *allegiance* to or *faith* in a dogma, or a word of god (or a tradition); and sometimes: a free *vital upsurge*.

Pray believe, dear friend, in my affectionate respect.

To Madeleine Slade

31 March, 1928

My Dear Friend,

I have just received your letter of 16 March; it presents my conscience with a real problem.

You know how joyful I should be to see Gandhi. But if the *main* object of Gandhi's visit to Europe is to see me, then I unhesitatingly say: 'No, it's *too much*. It isn't right. Indeed, it would be a bad thing if Gandhi were to interrupt his whole action in India to see me'.

Besides, I fear you may have given Gandhi an idea of me which isn't quite exact. I am, as everyone knows, deeply committed to ideas of peace and fraternal union among men, and when necessary I have sacrificed my own interests and tranquillity to them. But I'm not devoted *solely* to the cause of peace and social action.

I am on the one hand a profoundly religious being—in my own way, which is free. And on the other hand I'm a European intellectual and artist whose main efforts are directed towards the living comprehension of all human souls. I consider that my main role is to understand and enlighten,—to be a sort of archway linking together the minds of men and women, of peoples and races; *to understand all so as to love all*.

Here's an example to illustrate my case:

I have a great respect, an intellectual reverence for Goethe.

Can Gandhi admit such an attitude of mind?

Therefore I fear that if Gandhi comes to Europe for me, I may cause him a deep disappointment, and that I want to avoid at all costs.

But I know that a visit from him could be infinitely salutary and beneficial *to Europe*. And for myself—for my sister and I—it would be a very great joy.

I'm writing these lines in haste; take them as an expression of my need for absolute truth and my wish that Gandhi should decide knowing exactly what the situation is.

Ever yours,

Written from Villeneuve (Vaud), Villa Olga, Switzerland.

To Mahatma Gandhi

16 April, 1928

My Dear Friend,

Thank you for your letter of 30 March which I have just received.

I see you are still uncertain whether to come, and I fear my last letter may have added to your uncertainties rather than clarifying them. I wrote it in haste to catch the post, and I couldn't weigh my terms exactly. I wouldn't want it to be misunderstood.

Please understand that it was a moral scruple which drove me to write it, and rather than fall short, I was inclined to exaggerate that scruple. A sincere man like yourself knows how painful it is to risk giving an idea of oneself different from what one really is—*even* if it's superior to what one is—indeed, *above all* if it's superior. . .

I am not, as you are, a man whose inner forces are realized in action—though my action is always faithful to my thought. The essence of my life is rather to be found in thought. True and free thought is my commanding need, my vital necessity, and the role which has been given to me; I have never ceased to work towards it.

This need to know, to understand (and understanding is impossible without love), this perpetual drive for truth corresponds to a religious instinct within me, very deep, which was for a long time obscure, then in a sort of halflight, and has steadily become brighter. The closer I come to my end as an individual, the more I feel myself filled with God, and I realize this God in the particular field of beauty and truth. I know that He is far beyond this, but I touch Him, I taste Him, and I breathe His breath.

Thus my divine field (if I may so express it) is perhaps different from yours, though they touch. But they belong to the same Master: they are of His flesh.

However great would be my joy to see you and speak with you, I still believe that it would be neither right nor fair for you to come to Europe *solely for that*.

But it would be right and it would be fair for you to come to Europe in order to make contact with the youth of Europe, which needs your help, your advice and your enlightenment.

And *it is necessary* in either case (whether you come or not), it is indispensable that you should give an absolutely clear, precise and definitive formulation to the listening world of your doctrine, your faith, on the matter of war and non-acceptance.

We are both of us fairly old and of suspect health; we may disappear any day. It is important that we should leave a precise testament to the youth of the world which it can use as a rule of conduct, for it will have a terrible burden to bear in the coming half-century. I see fearful trials building up in front of them. It no longer seems to me a matter of doubt that there is in preparation an era of destruction, an age of global wars beside which all those of the past will seem only children's games, of chemical warfare which will annihilate whole populations. What moral armour are we offering to those who will have to face up to the monster which we shall not live to see? What immediate answer to the riddle of the murderous Sphinx, who will not wait? What marching orders?

Our words must not be equivocal. We have the sad example of Christ, whose admirable Gospels contain too many passages which, though not contradictory in fundamental content, at least appear so in form, and lend themselves to the self-interested interpretations of the worst Pharisees. In the last war we saw in all countries how hypocrites, fanatics, statesmen like Lloyd George, bishops and pastors, false believers and, worst of all, true believers, could by chosen passages from the New Testament justify themselves for extolling war, vengeance and holy murder. In the coming crises, there must be no doubt about Gandhi's thought.

Then again, it is necessary to weigh all the consequences of the orders given, to weigh the forces of the men to whom they will be entrusted.

The young men of Europe are aware of the trials waiting for them. They don't want to be duped about the imminence of the danger, which too many 'pacifists' are trying not to see and to put out of their minds. They want to look it clearly in the face, and they ask: 'To what extent is it *reasonable,* to what extent is it *human, not to accept*? Must the sacrifice be total, absolute, without exception, without any consideration either for ourselves or for the things which surround us and depend on us? And in all honesty to ourselves, can we be sure that this total sacrifice will diminish the sum total of future human sufferings—or does it not risk handing over man's destiny to a barbarity without counterweight?'

I'm asking the questions (some of the questions) which I feel are being turned over in the minds of the young. I'm not giving my own answers. I don't count. My importance in this matter is secondary alongside yours. The man of pure thought (pure in the intellectual sense) has no more than a weak effect on the present; his forecasts have only a long-term chance of working themselves out. But you as a man of active faith are the direct intermediary between the forces of Eternity and present movements. You are on the poop-deck; you have the power to give direct orders to the sailors how to steer the ship in the storm. Give those orders! Let's stop thinking about the port we have left (that 1914 war, about which we seem unable to reach understanding and which risks confusing all our discussions) and look to the port we must reach—in the future!

My dear friend, I'm sorry to be always speaking to you so freely. I am aware of my moral inferiority, I am not worthy to touch your feet. But I know the anxiety and the doubts which assail the best men in Europe, and I am passing on what they say.

                    Assuring you of my respectful affection,

Written from Villeneuve (Vaud), Villa Olga, Switzerland.

To MAHATMA GANDHI

                                              17 February, 1929

My Dear Friend,

We have been reading in *Young India* your reasons for giving up your trip to Europe this year. We understand them too well to think of countering them by reasons based on our own selfish affection—or even by those of the youth of Europe, threatened by new catastrophes, who could profit so much by your advice when they come to decide the route to follow and cut through their mortal hesitations.

But it is clear to me that your first duty is in India at this grave hour of vigil before the battle, for I have little doubt that this is the eve of the battle.

All I should like to do is to offer you a few reflections on the fearful days which India faces.

You know the conditions of modern combat. You know
that the first act of the modern state in warfare is to ruin its
adversary in the opinion of the rest of the world; to this end it
stifles its enemy's voice and fills the world with its own. You
know that the British Empire is past master in this art, and
that it has all the wherewithal to blockade India and cut her off
from the rest of the world, which it can then flood with its
own propaganda. The process has already started. For the
last month events in Bombay have served as a pretext for
making the world think that India is in flames, and every day
the main French papers, with docility which I suspect is
well-paid, receive the reports coming from England and
carry stories with large headlines about 'Hell in Bombay' and
the 'sinister tally' of each day—as if the trouble extended to
the whole of India and as if there were no evil, crimes or
massacres anywhere but in India—as if the salvation of all
humanity depended on the good gaoler keeping the prison
doors well bolted, to protect the world from the Indian hydra
which he alone in his heroism is able to keep in chains! It is
easy to imagine how shrill this propaganda will become as
the decisive hour approaches, and when the gauntlet is down
it will know no bounds.

Now I have already seen far too much evidence of the
terrifying intellectual passivity in which the peoples of
Europe are at present lying. Ever since the first day of the
1914 war their poor brains have been subjected to so much
daily intoxication from the whole of their press that they
have become unable to react. This is another type of
intellectual alcoholism, no less ravaging in its effects than the
other. There is hardly a free newspaper left in the West.
There is not one where a free man like myself can write
(except for a few poor news-sheets with no circulation and
one or two large reviews which do not reach wide public
because they appear at infrequent intervals and cost quite a
lot).

I consider it would be of urgent utility of India to take the
first step—before the blockade which awaits her—and have

her cause heard directly in Europe. I do not suggest that you take a stance of political 'mendicancy', as you call it, or that you ask for anyone's help. But in face of the tribunal of public opinion where the British Empire as plaintiff alone is heard, the defendant too must make herself heard, and become plaintiff in her turn. No one fights alone today. The whole world is involved in every conflict, and it throws the enormous weight of its opinion into one of the trays of the balance—either for or against. It was largely by this weight of opinion, well directed and well manipulated by the Allies, that the German Empire was crushed.

It would be unwise of the Indian leaders to neglect these great forces. It seems to me indispensable that they should use this year to prepare European opinion, to open the eyes of the thousands of men here who are blindfolded by their domesticated press. If you do not come yourself, other highly qualified Indian personalities should make themselves seen and heard in various countries of Europe and America. But the difficulty is to find such personalities whose name already represents in the world, as yours does, an uncontestable moral power, whose ascendency will force the crowds to listen and believe them. Alongside yourself, only Tagore enjoys this ascendency in Europe, and Tagore's health does not permit him much effort now. It should be your task to see who could be India's best legates in Europe. Anyway, do not neglect this form of action! And prepare straightaway, if you can, channels through which India can keep in communication with Europe, to be ready for the extremely likely contingency of communications being officially cut off by the British Government.

My dear friend, I send you my affectionate wishes for your health. Look after it, in view of tomorrow's great task for which your presence is indispensable.

Please believe in my respect and fraternal devotion.

Yours,

Written from Villeneuve (Vaud), Villa Olga, Switzerland.

To Sigmund Freud

17 July, 1929

Dear Great Friend,

I am much honoured to learn that the letter I wrote to you at the end of 1927 has prompted you to new researches, and that a new work will reply to the questions I had posed you. You have the full right to bring them before the wider public; and I would not wish to evade responsibility for them in any way.

I should only acknowledge that being at a distance of one year and a half, I no longer remember very exactly the text of my letter. I was then no doubt at the beginning of my long studies on the Hindu mind, which I am going to publish in a few months, in three volumes devoted to 'Mysticism and action in living India'. Since 1927 I have been able to delve deeply into that 'oceanic' sentiment, innumerable examples of which I find not only among hundreds of our contemporary Asians, but also in what I might call the ritualistic and multi-secular physiology which is codified in treatises on *yoga*. . .

At the end of my work, while reading, for comparison, some of the great mystics of Europe and particularly those of the Alexandrian epoch, those who lived in the West during the 14th century—not to speak of the considerable work of Abbé Brémond on French mysticism during the 16th and 17th centuries—I was surprised to observe, once again, that it is not at all true that the East and the West are two worlds separated from each other, but that both are the branches of the same river of thought. And I have recognized in both the same 'river ocean'. . .

It would be a pleasure for me to offer you my work when it is published: (the first volume next October; the second and the third in January).

Pray believe, dear great friend, in my affectionate respect.

Written from Rigi-Kaltbad.

To Albert Schweitzer

15 December, 1929

My Dear Friend,

All my best wishes for your forthcoming sojourn in
Lambaréné, and thanks for sending me your Autobiography.
How deeply do we regret that you were not able to visit us
for a little while, during your strenuous rest in Europe!
I am sending you the first volume of my work on the
mysticism and action in contemporary India. The next two
volumes are coming out towards the end of the month and I
shall have them forwarded to you. It is likely that you will be
interested more in them than in the first volume, because, of
the two great Indians I am speaking of, the second is the St
Paul of India: Vivekananda directed all the mystic forces of
his race towards active love and service of humanity.

Most affectionately yours,

Written to Albert Schweitzer, Gunsbach (Alsace), with a note to forward
to 2 Rue de Greniers, Strasbourg, from Villeneuve (Vaud), Switzerland.

To Pierre Herdner

14 July, 1930

. . . One must have faith, or otherwise not meddle with
such things at all. I shall never advise anyone who does not
have faith to take part in a movement of Passive Resistance at
a time when war has broken out. Because he must be
prepared to be sacrificed. I find some of your leaders severely
guilty, who keep you in illusion on this point and delude you
with the hope that the war will stop before folded arms. It
will stop—yes!— but after it has passed over the bodies of
those who obstructed its path. It will stop in the wake of

Villeneuve (Vaud) villa Olga

22 octobre 1932

à Gandhi

Cher ami que je vénère et que j'aime,

Nous avons reçu vos deux bonnes lettres du 16 et du 30 septembre. Merci d'avoir pensé à nous, en de telles heures!

Nous avons été auprès de vous, par la pensée, durant ces jours; et je n'ai pas besoin de vous dire que dans notre pensée il y avait une angoisse.

Mais je savais que vous aviez raison. Je savais que votre sacrifice était, non seulement grand, mais juste, légitime, et nécessaire. Il était votre mission, à cette heure décisive de votre peuple. Nulle cause ne l'exigeait, avec une force aussi impérieuse que cette cause des Intouchables. L'honneur de l'Inde, son unité

2 Letter from Romain Rolland to Mahatma Gandhi dated 22 October 1932.

world opinion, incensed at the sacrifice of Passive Resisters. It is the sacrifice which alone can bring—prepare—the coming victory of mankind, the salvation of future generations. But this sacrifice cannot be avoided. I beg your pardon for telling 'unpleasant truths'. But I cannot tolerate the insipid and dangerous optimism which leads to the worst disappointments. One must will and dare, but while looking straight in the face of what one is confronted with. None of you should be dragged unprepared into a heroic crusade in which he risks everything. For anyone to decide to do that, he must consider his own life less valuable than the salvation of the world. A small band of Passive Resisters, ready to undergo everything and conquer everything morally, is worth more than a numerous and unsure army which would take to flight at the first shock and accuse its chiefs of having deceived it.

As to the aptitudes of our Europe for Passive Resistance (which I call by a more energetic name: non-acceptance)— she has proved them for a long time. She did not wait for Tolstoy and Gandhi to practise the doctrine, which goes back to the early days of Christendom in the West. Just a few leagues away from my house, in the mountain pass of St Maurice en Valais, at the foot of the Dent Du Midi, was massacred the Legion Thébaine, martyr of Christian non-violence.

Tolstoy has a family of forerunners in Europe. One of the most remarkable of them was Peter Cheltschizki, the 15th century Hussite from Bohemia. His major book, *Das Netz des Glaubens*, has recently been republished in German, with a preface by President Masaryk.

But there is more: how can one forget that the heroic Poland of 1860 signed with her blood the gospel of non-violence—the 'Psalms of the future'—written by her great poet Krasinski? In 1861 the population of Warsaw let itself be shot down by the troops of Gortchakoff, without seeking to defend itself. Gortchakoff, exasperated, went on shouting at them in vain: 'Take up your arms! Fight!'

Krasinski sung: 'Must one be a murderer with the murderers, a criminal with the criminals? The world is crying to us: "At this price, to you the strength, to you the liberty! If not, then nothing!" No, my soul, no, not with these arms! Oh my country, be the unbending will, the humble contemplation, be the calm amidst the tempest; in your struggle against the hell of this world, be that force of calmness and love, before which hell in its totality will be powerless!'

Gortchakoff did not survive the shame which these massacres of a heroic and martyred people caused him. And the whole world trembled before the greatness of the sacrifice. Poland would never have resuscitated without the veneration which such examples imprinted on the heart of Europe.

You see that we do not need to go to Asia to recover non-acceptance. Europe, too, had its great moments of Passive Resistance. She is forgetful of her past and genius. Make them come to life again!

To Tetsuichiro Hasegawa

23 July, 1930

Dear Friend Hasegawa,

(I can give you this name, since during your stay at Villeneuve my sister and I have read, in your words and in your silence, the nobility of your soul and the seriousnes of your affection.)—I thank you for your kind remembrance, which touches us sincerely. We are grateful to Katayama for having brought you to the Villa Olga.

You speak of those hours spent together as a profound dream, which belongs neither to the East nor to the West, neither to the past nor to the future. It is true that we are living today a great dream of humanity, which perhaps was never before present on earth: it is the flower of a stormy spring, announcing a powerful future. Let us be happy and proud to take part in it, notwithstanding the tempests which assail us!

You are telling me that you will preserve and transmit to friends in Japan a little of the atmosphere which you have found in the Villa Olga. I am aware that this atmosphere is made partly of something which has been transmitted to me in my turn by the old France of Hugo and Renan, by the old Germany of Goethe and Beethoven, by the old Italy of Mazzini, friend of Malwida of Rome, by the old Russia of Tolstoy who responded to my appeal when I was a youth. I have added to it my own conquests—and my defeats, which are even more precious than the victories. Because there are times in this world when it is good to be defeated, but without bending one's head, nor kneeling down. Take, in your turn, my moral heritage, and enhance it! I hope it will come back, through you and my Indian friends, from Asia to Europe. At present, in the East as in the West, we have just one identical task. We work together. When one team grows weak, the other team takes over. Without a day of intermission, there rises up our common monument, our future cathedral of humanity.

I clasp your hand with all my heart. You now know the road to the Villa Olga; we shall expect to see you there again. Our friendly greetings to Katayama.

Affectionately yours,

Being away from Villeneuve, I have not yet seen—but my sister has described to me—the beautiful fans you have sent, for which we thank you very much.

Written from Park Hotel, Vitznau.

To Reginald Reynolds,

19 September, 1930

Dear Reginald Reynolds,

I was very pleased to receive your letter. I know you by your messages from India, which we received and which my sister read to me (unfortunately I do not read English well). We liked their forceful frankness, penetrating eye and sense of humour. Your have done good work, and I know from C. F. Andrews that you are carrying on in England. It is sad, but understandable, that the truth is having so much trouble to make itself known. The British economy has got so used to living off the exploitation of India that it has become almost impossible to break away from it without causing possibly mortal sufferings to the whole present social state. In these circumstances, people prefer to hide their heads under a stone, like the ostrich, and pretend that they see nothing. Which means that they'll be all the more harshly driven into the wall at the hour of reckoning; it's the '*Dike*' of iniquity. Once you're caught in its snare, you can't break away; you have to pay, and all too often the innocent pay for the guilty. I know that Gandhi's generous mind is concerned at this inextricable situation, and that he would have liked to spare England the material trials he foresees for her. But the blind ostrich won't let him.

I have the same conception of Peace as yourself. My motto, written at the head of the latest volume of my novel, *Mère et Fils*, is Spinoza's strong words:

Pax enim non belli privatio,
Sed virtus est, quae ex animi fortitudine oritur.

The 'pacifism' of 'good people' (it's not very much to be 'good people'! What we need is 'brave people') is fatal to all virtues, and above all else to energy, the mother of them all—energy of thought which does not evade the issue and dares to be sincere with itself—and energy of the will which dares to say what it believes to be true, and to act on what it says.

The emasculated 'pacifist' movement has allowed itself to be taken in by the deceptive mask of today's democratic states, who are ruining their peoples producing armaments for the most ferocious of wars. This mask must be torn away; no dealings are possible with hypocrisy! Frank violence is worth more than that; it is healthier even when it kills.

It is infinitely regrettable that your 'great leader' couldn't visit Europe, as he thought of doing in 1928, before beginning the great struggle for India. I wish he could have made contact with our best Europeans and worked out with them some principles for action, and above all means of applying them, appropriate to the conditions and character of the West. Maybe you could think about collecting and editing a Gospel of action for Europe, along with Andres, based on Gandhi's latest writings (his discussions in *Young India* and his continuing meditations, which seem to have matured and clarified his thought further over the last five or six years).

It's no use shutting him up in a prison; his spirit is and always will be present among those who know him—like the spirit of the Man who came to sit at table with his disciples in Emmaus. You will bear the reflection of his halo upon you for the whole of your life. Pass it on! That is your portion.

I shall send you a few words for Mahatmaji's birthday. Please add my name to yours on the telegram you send him. You could also add that of the venerable Paul Birukoff, the faithful friend and devout secretary of Tolstoy. This old man, so touching with serene faith amidst his trials, now lives in Onex near Geneva,—half paralysed and needing money. He always keeps Gandhi's portrait above his bed, facing that of Tolstoy. Make a point of sending him your excellent little brochure, and if you have any more copies available, please send a few to my sister, Madeleine Rolland (same address as mine). She could use them, on the one

hand for the archives of her Women's International League
for Peace and Liberty (French section), and on the other for
the 'French Satyagrahists'. In general it would be worthwhile
to send my sister the published documentation on India as it
appears (except *Young India*, which she takes regularly), as
she could pass it on in France to the small groups most eager
to help the cause.

I shake your hand heartily. Do believe me, dear Reginald
Reynolds.

Yours, brotherly,

Written from Villeneuve (Vaud), Villa Olga, Switzerland.

To Albert Einstein

12 October, 1930

Dear Great Friend,

I thank you cordially for your letter.

Nothing seems to me more appropriate to the celebration
of one of India's spiritual leaders than to express, as you wish
to do, our moral adhesion to the principle of non-acceptance
without violence, which in our civilization is translated into
the refusal of military service.

You know that this is my conviction as well. I should
merely like to be sure that we never forget, and we never let
those who listen to us forget, that in our violent Europe, on
the eve of a new attack of *delirium tremens*, this refusal has, or
will have self-sacrifice as a necessary consequence. Those
over whom we have spiritual charge must not be allowed to
form illusions on the strength of our words; they must realize
that we are leading them to almost certain martyrdom. If
they agree to this, then so do we. In our hard human life,
martyrdom is almost always the necessary stage through

which reason must pass in order to progress into the world of facts . . .

> Believe me, yours affectionately,

Written from Villeneuve (Vaud), Villa Olga, Switzerland when Einstein was still resident in Germany.

To Lucien Price

> 25 December, 1931

My Dear Friend,

I thank you for your letter of 11 December and for the trouble you have taken for the Goethe number of *Europe*. As a matter of fact, I only wanted from you some particulars for transmitting to the director of *Europe*, Jean Guéhenno, because it's he, and not me, who is organizing the number. (I have contented myself with writing for it an essay, the title and central thought of which are the great words of Goethe: '*Strib und werde*!' You'll read it.) I am writing therefore to Guéhenno asking him to get in touch with you and Mr Lewis Mumford directly. I've given him your address.

Your article in the *Globe* on our meeting with Gandhi touched me no less than your most welcome letter. I recognize in it your warm heart.

How pleased I would have been to have you here during our Indians' stay! They were here for five days, from Sunday evening to Friday 11th in the afternoon, staying in the Villa Lionnette. The little man, spectacled, toothless, enveloped in his white burnous, legs bare, skinny and stilt–like, like a heron's, head bare and tonsured with rough stubble damp in the rain, came up to me with a jerky laugh, his mouth open like a good dog panting. He rested his cheek on my shoulder, putting his right arm round me, and I felt his grey head against my cheek; the kiss of St Dominic and St Francis (hark at me boasting!). With him were Mira (Miss Slade), proud of features and with the august bearing of a Demeter, and three Indians, a young son of Gandhi called Devdas, with a round and happy face (a nice lad, not fully aware of the great name he bears), and two secretaries and disciples, young men of rare qualities of mind and heart: Mahadev Desai and Pyarelal.

Since I'd managed just before he came to pick up a bad cold on my chest, Gandhi came to me each morning in the first-floor room in the Villa Olga where I sleep (you remember it), and we had long conversations. (My sister served as interpreter, helped by Mira, and I also had a Russian friend and secretary, Marie Koudacheff, to note down our conversations. Schlemmer, our neighbour in Montreux, took some good photographs to capture the scene.) Then at 7:00 in the evening, in the ground-floor lounge, there were prayers, with the lights out, the Indians sitting on the floor, a little assembly of the faithful in a group round him: a series of three fine chants, the first taken from the *Gita*, the second an ancient hymn based on Sanskrit texts, translated by Gandhi, the third a canticle of Rama and Sita, intoned by Mira's grave and warm voice. These fine recitatives, unfolding calmly in the night, were separated by periods of total silence. Gandhi holds prayers again at 3:00 in the morning, for which he would wake up his hard-pressed staff in London when they'd only got back at 1 o'clock. He's an unbreakable little man, though he looks frail; tiredness is a word he doesn't know; he could spend hours answering every point thrown at him by a listening crowd attacking him, as he did in Lausanne and Geneva—sitting on a table, his voice staying clear and calm, striking back at both declared and undeclared adversaries (and there was no lack of them in Geneva!) with harsh truths which left them dazed and choking. The Swiss bourgeoisie, militarist and national-ist, which first received him with astute courtesy, was trembling with rage when he left, and I believe he would have been forbidden any more public meetings if his stay had been longer. He expressed himself in the clearest and most unequivocal terms possible on the double question of national armies and conflicts between capital and labour; I myself spurred him on considerably in this latter direction. His mind advances by successive experiments on action and he sticks to a straight course, but he never stops, and one could easily make mistakes if one judged him by what he said ten years ago, as his thought is in constant evolution. I'll give you just one typical example. He was asked in Lausanne to define what he meant by God. He explained how, among the thousands of names given to God in the Hindu scriptures, he settled in his youth on the word *Truth* as the most essential definition. So he said '*God is Truth*'. 'But', he adds, '*Two years ago* I went a step further, to say that "*Truth is God*".' For 'even the atheists do not doubt the necessity and the power of truth. In their passion to discover truth, the atheists have not hesitated to deny the existence of God, and, *from their point of view, they are right.*' This detail alone will give you a glimpse of the boldness and independence of this religious spirit of the East. I've noticed similar details in Vivekananda.

For his brief journey to Italy, I spent a long time putting him on his guard, and I sent him to one of my friends in Rome, General Moris, who made him his guest and kept him out of some of the traps. (N.B. There's no point in mentioning his name if you have occasion to speak about this in public; it would be held against Moris.) When he saw Mussolini, he took the precaution of having two witnesses with him, Mira and his secretary, to prevent his words from being deformed, and I'm sure he expressed himself with his usual liberty. Gandhi's account of his interview with the Duce, echoes of which have reached me, is full of humour; we'll talk about it again. In any case he hasn't been taken in; there's no political trick that can catch him out. His own policy is to say everything he thinks to anyone; there's never anything hidden. So the two Herculean policemen bestowed on him by England, who escorted him to Brindisi, swollen on the way by their Swiss and Italian counterparts, didn't earn their money—unless they forged false reports! (Of which there was no lack in the Fascist press.)

On the last evening, after the prayers, Gandhi asked me to play him a little Beethoven. (He doesn't know Beethoven, but he knows that Beethoven was the link between Mira and myself, and that I was then the link between Mira and him; thus in the end all our gratitude goes back to' Beethoven.) I played him the Andante from the *Fifth Symphony*, and I added Gluck's *Elysian Fields* (the orchestral piece and the flute melody). He is very affected by the religious chants of his country which are related to our finest Gregorian melodies, and he has worked to collect them. We also exchanged our ideas on *art*, a notion which he does not separate from that of *truth*, nor from that of *joy* which he says truth should bring. '*Sat-chit-ananda*'. . . '*Sat*' means 'truth'. '*Chit*' means 'that which lives' and 'true knowledge'. 'Ananda' means 'ineffable joy'. But it goes without saying that for his heroic nature joy is not found without effort, nor indeed without harshness. '*The seeker after truth has a heart tender as the lotus and hard as granite.*'

These, my dear friend, are just a few shreds from these last few days, of which I have taken detailed notes. What I haven't told you about is the whirlwind of tiresome, curious and half-mad creatures let loose on our villas as a result of his passage. The telephone never stopped ringing, photographers in ambush were letting fly from every bush. The Lake of Geneva Dairymen's Union wrote that they hoped to be '*purveyors*' to the 'king of India' while he was staying with me. We had letters from 'sons of God'; and there were Italian women writing to the Mahatma to ask him for ten numbers for the next draw in the '*Lotto*' (the weekly national lottery)!

My sister, overworked, has gone to Zurich for ten days of rest and cure. She is coming back tomorrow. As for me, I've almost lost my sleep. If you find it send it back to me, by registered post!

I really must finish this letter. A lot of arrears of work to

catch up. For the New Year, dear friend, I embrace you with
all my heart. May the year be good to us! Even if it is hard,
I'll call it good if it spares us our health. The rest is our
business. No struggle frightens us.

Fraternally to you and Fred,

Written to Lucien Price in the USA from Villeneuve (Vaud), Villa Olga,
Switzerland.

To Albert Schweitzer

23 September, 1932

Dear Friend,

I am rather reluctant to take charge of the appeal which
your friends in Geneva, and notably the Claparèdes, want me
to address to you. Because I myself am besieged with similar
appeals, and like you, overburdened with work, and like you
(I hope: more than you), ill, I am annoyed with those who
bother me.

But the present occasion is so serious—serious for all of us
Europeans—that I have no hesitation in writing to you.

You know that at the beginning of October (6 October)
we are organizing in Geneva an international day for Gandhi.
The point is not the man, nor India either. It is the cause
which he represents, the outcome of which, victorious or
disastrous, may decide the destiny of Europe for a century or
more—the non-violence, or to be more precise, *organized and
collective non-acceptance without violence.*

For several years now, I have been in close touch with
social movements in the world, particularly in the USSR and
in Asia. I know what wrath and what expectations Indian
Satyagraha gives rise to. I know that this heroic and patient
experiment of a people, led by a 'Judge of Israel', is the

unique and ultimate dam which still resists the enormous waves of accumulated violence. Because, apart from a violent revolution, it is the only strong and effective instrument for achieving the social transformation, or rather, the sudden change, which is inevitable and urgent. If Gandhi fails, the torrent will run wild over all the earth. And I will be the first to cry out to it: 'Break loose!' Because, whatever the cost, the social situation of today has to be swept away. And it will be.

Don't you think that at this perhaps most crucial moment (for I still do not know whether Gandhi will go up to the end of his sacrificial decision—his fast unto death) we must make our voice heard in favour of the man who will perhaps take away with him, in the event of his death, the last hope for peace in our torn times?

In the absence of your physical presence in Geneva, try, try, I beg you, to send a message, as I will do! And if you can join the International Committee for Gandhi, or do anything else for the cause using your personal connections, please do it!

I clasp your hands with all my heart.

                                                  Your old friend,

I was seriously ill this summer (intestinal lesions). I am recovering with difficulty. But the work is not suffering.

Written from Villeneuve (Vaud), Villa Olga, Switzerland.

TO MAHATMA GANDHI (Telegram)

                                                  27 September, 1932

Happy for your great spiritual victory.

To Mahatma Gandhi

22 October, 1932

My Dearly Beloved and Revered Friend,

We received your two kind letters of 16 and 30 September. Thank you for thinking of us at such a time!

We were with you in thought during those days, and I don't need to tell you that our thoughts were full of anxiety.

But I *knew* that you were right. I *knew* that your sacrifice was not only great, but just, legitimate and necessary. It was your mission at this decisive hour for your people, and no cause demanded it more imperiously than that of the untouchables. The honour of India, her moral unity which is the essential kernel of all social and political unity, her very right to exist and to live again, are at stake in this preliminary reparation made to the victims of an outdated social order, this re-acceptance into the fold of millions of brothers who had been driven out. The whole of humanity has an interest in the results of the '*great experiment*' which you are directing, and no one, not even you, can know the results in advance. We can but wait for them and believe, as the '*great experiment*' unfolds itself according to the strict laws of Truth—like science.

But on these results depend the destiny of the world and the shape of future action in it, and only the success of the '*Satyagraha*' experiment can save humanity from the torrents of violence hanging over it. We must pray, and the true prayer is the one which, like yours, is offered in the midst of action.

My sister and I send you our warmest thoughts of love and respect. Please pass on our friendly greetings to those of your companions at Villeneuve who are with you now.

Yours,

I am sending you in another package the copy of a message by me about you which was read to a pro-Indian assembly in Geneva.

Written from Villeneuve (Vaud), Villa Olga, Switzerland.

To Mahatma Gandhi

2 May, 1933

My Dear and Revered Friend,

We are with you in these grave days when again your life is at stake. We hope ardently that the hardness of heart of those of your people who are blocking the great work of national reparation to the Untouchables will finally give way. Let them tremble at the prospect of assuming in the eyes of history the execrable responsibility of causing your death! They would bear the mark on their brow in the memory of mankind for evermore.

But allow me to read in your sacrifice an even broader meaning than that of the Untouchables cause! At this tragic moment of history, when the whole world is exposed to the most atrocious violence, on the eve of world wars surpassing in cruelty and extent all that have gone before,—a moment when the whole of humanity is divided between oppressors and oppressed, and when the latter, maddened by their sufferings and by injustice, as if drunk by the violence which rends them, see no other recourse than in that very violence,—your self-immolation to that sacred Justice which is all love and no violence takes on a universal and holy value,—like the Cross.

Though, alas! the Cross has not saved the world, it has shown the world the way to save itself, and its rays have cast light on the night of millions of unfortunate people.

. . . But let us hope that we are spared this sacrifice today! May you remain a long time—I will not say among us (for I doubt whether my own sickness-ridden life will last much longer), but among our brothers and sisters in India and the whole world who need your presence on board to guide the ship in the storm.

Give me your blessing, and my sister Madeleine!

I embrace you affectionately,

P.S. Fraternal greetings to our dear guests in Villeneuve, to your brood: our sister Mira, Devdas (whose letter we received), Mahadev Desai and Pyarelal. I often think of them.

Written from Villeneuve (Vaud), Villa Olga, Switzerland.

TO KALIDAS NAG

24 December, 1933

Dear Friend,

I cannot write to you as I would have liked to. The crushing multitude of my tasks, all the questions, all the appeals to which, almost daily, I must reply, and my own work which I persist in pursuing, in snatching away, bit by bit, from the onslaught of a voracious world, forbid me almost totally any gentle relaxation amidst friends.

But I never forget you. I converse with you, often, in my thought.

I have finished the work I have been glued to for twelve years (it was in 1921 that I had started it): *L'Ame Enchantée*. The last volumes have come out. I will send them to you. They contain a second *Foire sur la Place* of France and the world, more terrible than the first one; and the final illumination, in the death of my hero, is more 'disenchanted', more freed from the bonds of life, than that of Christophe. But I think you will find me, on many pages, even closer to the soul of India and of yourself, and that you will faithfully accompany my Annette and her Marc till the end. You will shortly receive the three volumes of *Annonciatrice* if the postal service is normal.

My sister must have told you that Soumyendranath Tagore called on me. In spite of the excessive nature of his ideas, this young man evoked in me much esteem and sympathy, though mixed with pity (he has caught tuberculosis rather badly, I am told; and the trials awaiting him will

in no time ruin his delicate health). He would have liked to
involve me in his party, and he judges our friend, the saint of
Sabarmati, with an unrelenting violence, which seems to me
to mask an ill will based on injured love; since he once did
love the man passionately, and now cannot forgive him for
disappointing him. I need not tell you that I firmly held on to
my faith and hope in G. We debated for long, in words and
writing, without any result, as each of us remained inflexible.
He had written down an account of our discussion which he
wanted to publish, and loyally, he sent it on to me for
checking. For all his efforts · to be objective, he assigned
himself the good role, and sacrificed mine. I rewrote all my
answers (without touching his) and returned to him the text
thus transformed, telling him that it was the only one that I
would acknowledge as authentic. Loyally, he accepts it and
promises to me that he will publish the version corrected by
me. In the event of any controversy arising in India,
regarding the true meaning of my thought, I (or in my
absence, my sister Madeleine) would place at your disposal
copies of the categorical letters I have written to Soumyendranath.

(Between us, however, I wish the social thought of G.
would take shape, more and more. The hour is approaching
when, everywhere in the world, people will have to decide to
espouse one or the other of the two causes, or to leave
political action and retire to the forest. . .)

Soumyendranath has requested me earnestly to write to
the Poet (his uncle, I think), to put him on his guard against the
Hitlerian Fascism, emissaries of which, I hear, are regularly
prowling around Santiniketan. I do not want to do it
directly, I would be afraid of being indiscreet. I have already
been one of the causes responsible for making the Poet lose
his Italian friends, by opening his eyes to the way his great
name was being exploited by the Fascism of Mussolini. I
would be sorry to deprive him of his German friendships as
well. However, he should not let himself be exploited by the
self-seeking flatteries of official or officious representatives of

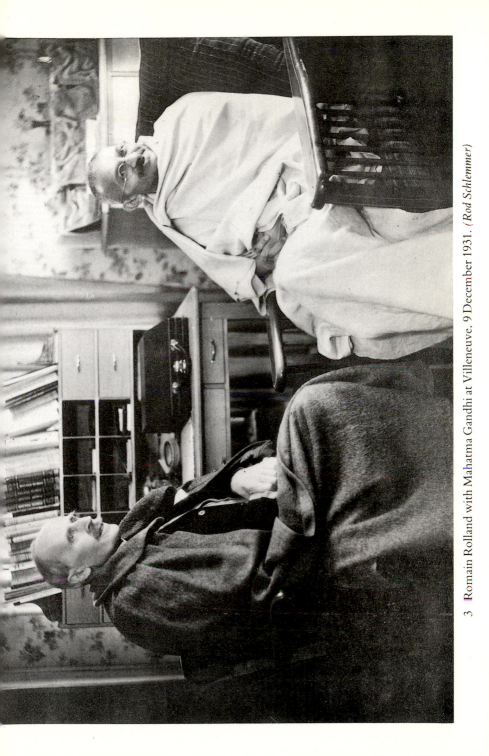

3 Romain Rolland with Mahatma Gandhi at Villeneuve, 9 December 1931. (*Rod Schlemmer*)

Hitlerism. Nazi propaganda, which is better organized, would very much like to utilize the pure flag of the Poet's idealism for hiding its abominable 'racism', which is nothing but a narrow and hallucinated sub–nationalism aiming at the domination and oppression of all the other races on earth. We in the West are in a better position to see the indescribable cruelties of the régime, to which thousands of refugees are witnesses, many of them fugitives from the bloody prisons and concentration camps of Germany. In the absence of those direct and trembling witnesses, I wish one could read in India a good complete translation of Hitler's *Mein Kampf*, which is the official breviary of millions of Germans. One cannot imagine anything breathing a more deadly hatred and a narrower, more inhuman, more ignorant fanaticism. All the current protestations of the government in the name of peace are only a farce to hoodwink its enemies; and Hitler himself has tactlessly unveiled in *Mein Kampf* his political Machiavell- ism. One must therefore be extremely cautious and remem- ber that (apart from old Gerhardt Hauptmann who, because of the weakness of his character, has always been, for the last twenty years, the 'poet–laureate' attached to the golden chain of the masters of the day, whoever they may be) all the great German writers have taken refuge outside of Germany and are opposed to the régime: Thomas Mann, Stefan Zweig, Hermann Hesse, etc. As for me, my new books are for- bidden in Germany, and even the Swiss houses who wanted to publish them are under the threat of boycott by Germany. The worst is that they have have been forbidden to publish even my old collection of articles, *Au-dessus de al mêlée*! The printers have been ordered to pulp the printed sheets.

I have written a number of protestations with regard to the persecutions of Jews, the burning of books and the Leipzig court case. I have also addressed one such protestation to the youth of India, to open their eyes to the dangers of Hitlerian propaganda. I do not know whether Madeleine has sent you a copy of it. In any case, sooner or later, its echoes will reach your ears.

When you talk to the Poet, tell him about my feelings on this subject, while conveying at the same time my profound affection for him.

Goodbye, dear friend. My old body is quite eaten up by enemies within; but it is valiant enough, and will try to hold its own for a few more years, until the hoped-for day of your crossing the threshold of my house again.

With my respectful remembrances to your wife and my faithful affection for you,

Written from Villeneuve (Vaud), Villa Olga, Switzerland.

To Jawaharlal Nehru

25 February, 1936

Dear Friend,

My ill-health has prevented me from coming to greet you before your departure. I wanted at least to send you, while we were still neighbours, our affectionate good wishes to you, your wife, and your dear country.

I am thinking of the emotion, for you, of this separation. May the coming spring improve the health of Madame J. Nehru and may you return, with a calmer spirit, to the great fight which awaits you over there.

I hope that under your guidance India, like our West, will know how to form a 'Popular Front' to fight against all obstacles to her independence and her social progress.—It is entrusted to me to ask you, as well as Gandhi, to join a Universal Assembly for Peace, which we are convening towards the end of this summer, probably in September, at Geneva. It will be a vast and powerful Congress, a sort of mobilization of all the forces in the world for peace. A number of great national and international organizations and personalities from France, England, United States, Czechoslovakia, Spain, Belgium, Holland and many other countries have already joined. (In England, Lord Robert Cecil, Major Attlee, Norman Angell, Philip Neel Baker, Alexander, Professor Lasky. In France, Herriot, Pierre Cot, Jouhaux, Cadrin, Racamond, Professor Langevin, etc. In Czechoslovakia, Benes, Hodza. In Spain, Azana, Alvarez del Vago, etc. In Belgium, Louis de Brouckere, Henri Lafontaine, etc.) It will be a question of organizing, simultaneously on a national and international level, resistance against the catastrophic menace of a universal conflagration. Would you please talk about this to our friends in India, while conveying to them my cordial salutations? Their reply as well as yours can be sent either to me or to the head office of the '*World Committee for the Struggle against War and Fascism*', of which I was made Honorary President (237 rue Lafayette, Paris X).

I wish it were possible for us to remain in regular communication with you and our Indian friends. It is important that western opinion is kept constantly informed of social and political developments in India, about which too many people are interested in preserving silence or spreading false news.

I clasp your hands whole-heartedly. Look after yourself, my dear friend, be happy, and may your cause, which is that of the best India, triumph!

Yours sincerely,

Once again, please give my affection to Gandhi and his friends who were our guests at Villeneuve,—to Mira, to Pyarelal and to Mahadev Desai.

I read with great interest your article which appeared in *Vendredi* with an introduction by Madame Andrée Viollis.—The other article you sent to my sister will come out in the March issue of the review, *Europe*.

Written from Villeneuve (Vaud), Villa Olga, Switzerland.

To Devdas Gandhi

2 December, 1936

My Dear Friend,

You know how much I love and honour India; she must resume the great place of seniority which belongs to her in the world's social and moral life. My fervent wish is that she may win back her national independence and achieve the social progress to which her huge people, so long sacrificed, has a right. Please pass on my warmest expression of this wish through your paper to Congress and to the Indian masses.

Unfortunately, I cannot write you an article at present. All our forces in Europe are absorbed by the tragic events in Spain and the threat of war weighing over the whole of the West—the whole of Europe. I am sending you a copy of an Appeal which I am sending to every people in aid of the victims of the Madrid massacres. India should at least learn something from the spectacle of the follies and crimes under whose weight Europe is succumbing. She must become aware of the mortal danger in imperialist and racialist Fascisms, which carry the torch of war everywhere and crush every liberty. India is not immune from their tortuous and rapacious politics, which aspire to nothing less than complete world domination. Beware of the German-Italian-Japanese Pact! Asia has suffered much under European imperialism, but those of yesterday still had to take account of certain legal principles written into their democratic nations. Those of tomorrow, founded by Fascist movements, will trample underfoot the last traces of humanity. We in France, over the last two years, have given up our party political quarrels (socialists, Communists, radical republicans, Catholic democrats, etc.) to form a Popular Front alliance against Fascism. I call upon you to do the same in India. All over the world, liberty and progress—our great hopes, our reasons for living—are in danger!

To Rabindranath Tagore

5 December, 1937

Very Dear Friend,

We have just read with emotion in the *Harijan* the news of your recent illness and of your visit—when hardly convalescent—to Mahatmaji who is also ill. Our thoughts were with you, mingled with a tender veneration for you both. I hope you have regained your health, and that your radiant light will be preserved for a long time yet to this poor world over which menacing shadows are gathering.

In the Bulletin of the Indian Civil Liberties Union, which I receive from time to time, I read your great name always in the frontline of the sacred struggle for the defence of liberty and for justice.

You know that in the West I take part in the same battles, which are still more desperate: for the circle of enemies is fiercer and draws closer every day. But the awakening (social, moral and intellectual) of the workers and peasants of France is a joy and a great hope for me. Especially since the last two or three years they have become conscious of their unity and strength, as well as of their duty towards humanity at large. I would wish them to have a powerful political guide like Jaures and a great poet like Victor Hugo—or like yourself. They deserve it.

In spite of my bad health—very carefully watched over by my two affectionate guardians, my wife and my sister,—I had the 'good fortune of never having had to interrupt my work up till now. I have published lately a new volume of my Beethoven Studies, which I have called *The Song of Resurrection*, (dealing with the period of crisis which brought forth the last sonatas and the 'Missa Solemnis' of Beethoven). And I am busy with new drama of my Cycle of the French Revolution –*Robespierre*, which marks the broken pinnacle of the pyramid. Whilst writing it, how many a tragic problem of our times do I encounter!

In which of your books has the beautiful poem appeared, which was inspired by the death of Pearson, and of which I read some fragments in the *Harijan*? It touched me deeply.

Will you convey my affectionate remembrance to your son and daugher-in-law, whose passing through here will never be effaced from our hearts; but the beautiful Hotel Byron, where they and you had put up, no longer exists. It is burnt down. It is now a huge deserted esplanade above the lake, surrounded by a circle of big trees—fruit-trees and cedars and wellingtonias.

I also address my cordial salutation to our dear Kalida Nag who I hope keeps good health. Pray be assured, my dear friend, of my faithful and profound affection.

We are leaving Switzerland next year. My mind no longer feels free enough here. I shall return to France where I have purchased in my Burgundy a small landed property on the ancient hill of Vezelay, where Saint Bernard preached the second crusade, and which is crowned by one of the most beautiful romano-gothic cathedrals of France.

We hope to be installed there in summer.

Written from Villeneuve (Vaud), Villa Olga, Switzerland.

To Rabindranath Tagore

27 February, 1940

Dear Great Friend,

My sister was with me, at Vezelay, where we received the letter announcing the marriage of your grand-daughter; we were happy to hear of it and we send you our congratulations and our very affectionate wishes.

I have not been able to write to you for a long time but my friendship remains faithful to you and my thoughts often visit you.

You know that I have left Switzerland since two years, and that I am installed with my wife in an old city of the 13th century, which has an epic past and which from its rock crowned by a dominating basilica, overlooks a vast circle of the meadows, woods and hills of Burgundy and Morvan. It had seen, in the olden days, Saint Bernard preaching the Second Crusade, and the Kings of France and England: Phillippe-Auguste and Richard *Cœur-de-lion* enlisting for the Holy Land. Formerly great and flourishing, the city now lies dying within the precincts of its old medieval walls. It is there, on these walls, above the patrol way, that my house is situated. From my bed I see the sun rise far away on the hills.

The war has created a solitude around us. Communications are not easy, especially in winter. The nearest railway station is about ten kilometres away, but we have kept our motor car, and the radio connects us with the rest of the world. Unable to write in the newspaper, which the state of war does not permit, I work and write for happier days. I re-live and try to fix on paper my memoires of the past century,—the days of my youth, and the first struggles, before 1900.

I hope you are keeping good health and that your days and nights are bathed in the sacred flame of poetry.

In a world handed over to blind violence and falsehood, we must preserve within us truth and peace.

Believe me, dear great friend, yours with brotherly affection,

P. S. Kindly convey my kind remembrances to all your family.

It is long since we have had any news of our dear common friend, Kalidas Nag. We are anxious.

Written from Vezeley (Yonne), 14, Grand rue, France.

CHRONOLOGY

1861	7 May: Birth of Tagore at Calcutta.
1863	Birth of Vivekananda.
1864	International Red Cross founded by Henri Dunant.
1866	29 January: Birth of Romain Rolland in Clamecy (Nièvre), son of Emil Rolland, a notary, and Antoinette-Marie Courot, the daughter of a notary.
1869	Opening of the Suez Canal.
	2 October: Birth of Mohandas Karamchand Gandhi at Porbandar.
1870	Franco-Prussian War.
1871	Third Republic in France.
1872	Birth of Madeleine, sister of R. Rolland. Having obtained an advanced degree in English, she served as translator and interpreter for her brother, notably during his conversations with Tagore and Gandhi.
1873–80	Romain Rolland attends the Collège de Clamecy.
1877	Dwijendranath Tagore publishes the newspaper *Bharati*.
1878–80	Tagore studies in London.
1880	The Rolland family leaves Clamecy for Paris.
1881	Vivekananda meets Ramakrishna.
1882	Romain Rolland begins his diary.
1883	During travels in Switzerland, Romain Rolland meets Victor Hugo.
	First session of the National Conference at Calcutta.
1885	First session of the Indian National Congress held at Bombay.
1886–9	Student at the Ecole Normale Supérieure in Paris, R. Rolland visits Renan, Writes to

Tolstoy (letter 1) who answers (4 October 1887). Passes his *agrégation* in history.

1889–91   Gandhi studies in London.

Romain Rolland studies at the Ecole française de Rome. He visits Italy and becomes friends with the aging German idealist Malwida von Meysenbug. He writes his first plays on themes of the Italian Renaissance and has an initial conception of Jean-Christophe. He travels to Bayreuth and returns to Paris.

1892   Marriage to Clotidle Bréal, daughter of the philologist Michel Bréal, professor at the Collège de France. His sister-in-law, Louisette Guieysse, later founded an Association of the Friends of Gandhi and edited the *Nouvelles de l'Inde* in Paris.

1892   Second trip to Italy to prepare his theses, returning thereafter to Paris. Writes *Niobé le siege de mantoue*.

1893   Swami Vivekananda attends Parliament of Religions at Chicago.

1893–1914   Gandhi in South Africa.

1895   Granted a *docteur-ès-lettres* for his two theses: *The Origins of Modern Lyric Theatre: A History of Opera Before Lully and Scarlatti; Cur ars Picturae apud Italos XVI Saeculi Deciderit.*

November: Teaches a course in Art History at the Ecole Normale Supérieure.

Writes two plays: *Saint Louis* (first published play, in *La Revue de Paris*, March–April 1897), and *Jeanne de Piennes* (unpublished).

1897   *Aert* (published in *La Revue d' Art Dramatique*, March–May 1898) is performed in the Théâtre de l'Oeuvre, 3 May 1898, by Lugné-Poe.

1898   Dreyfus Affair.

The affair was in part the inspiration for *Les*

Loups, the play that inaugurates his cycle on the Revolution. Performed at the Théâtre de l'Oeuvre, 18 May, and published by Péguy under the title *Morituri* under the pseudonym Saint-Just, ed. Georges Bellais.

1898	For the *Revue de Paris* and the *Revue d'Art Dramatique*, R. Rolland writes articles (later reprinted in *Le Theatre du Peuple*, 1903), and publishes *Le Triomphe de la Raison* (1899) performed at the Théâtre de l'Oeuvre, as well as *Danton*.
1899–1902	The Boer War.
1900	First Congress on the history of Music organized by R. Rolland.
1901–3	Feburary: Divorce. He takes an apartment at 162, boulevard Montparnasse. Contributes to the *Revue Musicale*. Publishes in the *Cahiers de la Quinzaine*, founded by Péguy: *Danton, le 14 Juillet* (1902), and *Le Temps Viendra*, manuscript inspired by the Boer War (1903).
1902	(until 1911): Gives courses in the history of music at the Ecole des Hautes Etudes Sociales. *Millet*, London, Duckworth.
1903	With the *Vie de Beethoven*, published in the *Cahiers de la Quinzaine*, he inaugurates his series of lives of famous men. He begins to compose *Jean-Christophe* which is serialized in the *Cahiers de la Quinzaine* between July 1903 and October 1912.
1904	November: Inaugural lecture in the History of Music at the Sorbonne.
1905	Receives the *Prix de la Vie heureuse*. Partition of Bengal.
1906	*La vie de Michel Ange, Cahiers de la Quinzaine*.
1908	*Musiciens d'Aujourd' Hui*, Hachette; *Musiciens d' Autrefois*, Hachette.
1910	20 November: Death of Tolstoy.

	After a serious accident, the convalescing Romain Rolland rereads Tolstoy, intending to write a article for *La Revue de Paris*.
	Haendel, Alcan.
1911	*Vie de Tolstoi*, Hachette.
1912	Abandons professional life and devotes his time to writing.
	End of the serial publication of *Jean-Christophe*.
1913	Publishes the *Tragedies de la Foi*, Hachette.
	Writes *Colas Breugnon*.
	13 June: *Grand prix de littérature de l'Académie française*.
	December: Reads *l'Offrande Lyrique* (Gitanjali) by Tagore, translated by André Gide, published by N.R.F.
	Tagore receives the Nobel prize for Literature.
	World War I.
1914–18	15 March: Moves to 3, rue Boissonnade, Paris.
1914	August: In Switzerland at the moment of the declaration of World War I, Romain Rolland, who is exempted from military service, does not return to France.
	22–23 September: 'Au-dessus de la Mêlée' published in a supplement to the *Journal de Geneve*.
3 Oct. 1914–3 July 1915:	Serves the International Agency of Prisoners of War founded by Dr Ferrière of the Red Cross.
1915	First encounter with India: exchange with A. Coomaraswamy *Au Dessus de la Mêlee*, Ollendorff.
	Gandhi arrives in India. Establishes the Satyagraha Ashram in Ahmedabad.
1916	Contributes to the review *Demain* founded by H. Guilbeaux in Geneva. These articles are later gathered together in *Les Precurseurs*.
	February: Battle of Verdun.

15 May: F. van Eeden, 'A Mes amis de
l'Orient et de l'Orient et de l'Occident,'
Demain, I, 15 May (poem dedicated to
Romain Rolland).

18 June: R. Tagore: 'India's Message to
Japan.'

2 November: To his article 'Aux peuples
assassinés,' Romain Rolland appends the
text of Tagore: *Message de l'Inde au Japon*.

13 November: Nobel Prize for Literature for
1915. R. Rolland gives the prize money to
humanitarian groups such as the Red
Cross.

1917 Beginning of the correspondence with Gorki.
Bose Research Institute established at
Calcutta.

1 May: 'A la Russie libre et libératrice,' in *Salut a
la Revolution Russe*

The October Revolution in Russia. Lenin as
head of the Council of Peoples'
Commissars in the USSR.

1918 15 May: 'Pour l'Internationale de l'Esprit:
"Elargissons l'humanisme!" ' in *Revue
Politique Internationale*.

15 April: 'Empédocle d'Agrigente et l'Age de la
haine,' Geneva, *Les Cahiers du Carmel*,
translated immediately into Bengali.

1919 10 April: first letter to Tagore (Letter 6)
May: Called back to Paris to the bedside of his
mother, who dies on 19 May. 'I owe to her
the best of myself: music and faith.'

26 June: 'Déclaration d'indépendance de
l'Esprit,' in *l'Humanite*. Manifesto signed
by more than one thousand intellectuals
and writers from around the world,
including Tagore, Coomaraswamy, and A.
Chakravarty.

28 June: Treaty of Versailles.
On the Treaty of Versailles, R. Rolland later

remarked. 'A sad peace. A mocking
intermission between two massacres. But
who thinks of tomorrow?'
Colas Breugnon, Ollendorff.
Liluli, Geneva: Le Sablier.
Voyage Musical Aux Pays du Passe, E. Joseph.
Les Precurseurs, éd. de l'Humanité.
League of Nations founded.

1920   August: Visit of D. K. Roy.
Clerambault, Ollendorff; *Pierre et Luce*, Geneva:
Le Sablier.

1921   19–21 April: First conversations with Tagore in
Paris. Begins to write *L'Ame Enchantee*
which is serialized from 1922 to 1933.
La Revolte des Machines, Geneva: Le Sablier.

1921–2   Controversy with Barbusse and the group
'Clarté' (see letters 9 and 10).
Les Vaincus, Antwerp, Lumière.

1922   January: 'Homage to Siva,' preface to Ananda
Coomaraswamy's *The Dance of Siva*.
10 March: Gandhi is arrested. Tagore
establishes Visvabharati University at
Santiniketan.
April: Visit of K. Nag.
The Chauri-Chaura incident leads to
Gandhi's suspension of the non-
cooperation movement.
30 April: Leaves Paris for Villeneuve,
Switzerland.
17–20 August: Visit of D. K. Roy.
February: Founding of the review *Europe*.
February–May: 'Mahatma Gandhi' appears in
Europe I (Feb.–May), a text later included
in the book *Mahatma Gandhi*.
September: Visit of K. Nag, of Pearson.

1924   21 January: Death of Lenin.
27 January: Visit of Paul Richard.
5 February: Gandhi, after an operation, is set
free.

30 March: Visit of F. D. Pocha.

'Paroles de Renan à un adolescent,' *Europe, IV*.

'l' Inde depuis la libération de Gandhi,' *Europe IV*, reprinted later as an afterword in the 21st edition of *Mahatma Gandhi*.

Mahatma Gandhi, Stock.

Introduction to 'La Jeune Inde,' in *La Revue Europeene, IV*.

Begins to write le Voyage Intérieur.

June: Visit of K. O. Kohli.

4 July: Conversation with L. L. Rai.

26 July: Visit of Paul Richard with his son, of Hirasawa, H. Alavi, A. Yasunghani and R. Naidu.

28 July: Visit of L. L. Rai.

17 August: Visit of Paul Richard, R. Naidu, K. J. Kabraji and Miss Hinde.

1925   January: Visit of Sudhindra N. Ghose.

18–19 February: Visit of L. K. Elmhirst.

July: Visit of Paul Richard.

14 September: Visit of Madeleine Slade.

Dictatorship of Benvenuto Mussolini.

'Music and Life,' translated by K. Nag, *Visva Bharati Quarterly, III*.

Introduction to Tagore, 'A Quatre voix' (Caturanga), translated by Madeleine Rolland, *La Revue Europeene, 12*.

Le Jeu de l' Amour et de la Mort, Geneva: Le Sablier.

1926   Sixtieth birthday of Romain Rolland: publication of a *Liber Amicorum* containing, among others, tributes from Gandhi and Tagore, and publication of a special issue of the revue *Europe*.

Pâques-Fleuries, which later serves as the Prologue to *Theatre de la Revolution*.

20 May: Visit of Nehru and his daughter Indira.

31 May: Visit of Lala Lajpat Rai.

22 June – 4 July: Tagore at Villeneuve. Series of conversations with R. Rolland.

15 August: 'Extraits des lettres de R. Tagore à diverses personnes,' *Europe, XI*.

5 September: Visit of K. T. Paul.

11 September: Visit of Ramananda Chatterjee.

4 October: Visit of Dhan Gopal Mukerji.

13 October: Visit of Jawaharlal Nehru, Nehru's sister and brother-in-law, Mr and Mrs R. S. Pandit.

1927   March: Trip to Vienna to commemorate Beethoven's Centennial.

Begins to write *Beethoven, les Grandes Édoques Créatrices* which is serialized from 1928 to 1943.

11 April: Visit of K. N. Narayana of Collengode.

29 April: Visit of R. M. Pratap.

1 May: Visit of Nehru.

13 May: Visit of Josephine MacLeod.

9 July: Visit of Jagadish Chandra Bose and Lady Bose.

24 October: Visit of D. K. Roy.

24 November: Begins writing *La Vie de Ramakrishna*.

30 December: Visit of M. Lal Bose and A. S. Raj.

1928   *Les Leonides*, play used as an epilogue to *Theatre of the Revolution*.

10 May: Visit of Ambalal Sarabhai.

15 July: 'La Réponse de l'Asie à Tolstoy,' *Europe, XVII*, text reused later in *The Life of Tolstoy*, Hachette.

7 August: Visit of Rajendra Prasad and Bhai-Balmukand.

29 August: Visit of Rathindranath and Pratina Tagore.

30 August: Visit of Boshi Sen.

3 September: Visit of J. C. Bose and Lady Bose.

16 September: Visit of C. F. Andrews.

17 November: Death of Lala Lajpat Rai.

December: 'Adresse au Congrès National de toute l'Inde,' *Europe, XVIII*.

'*L'Inde en marche*,' *Europe, XVIII*, extract from Prophets of the New India.

'Vivekananda and Paul Deussen,' *Funfzehntes Jahrbuch der Schopenhauergesellschaft*, extract from *Prophets of the New India*.

1929   Other extracts of *Prophets of the New India* published in *Europe, XIX, XX, XXI*.

Letter to the editor in *Asia, XXIX*.

27 October: Visit of Manilal Patel.

2 December: *The Life of Ramakrishna*, Stock.

December: Lahore Congress. Resolution passed by the Indian National Congress declaring compelete independance for India.

1930   20 January: *The Life of Vivekananda and the Universal Gospel*, Stock.

26 January: First Independence Day observed.

Preface to Lala Lajpat Rai, *L' Inde Malheureuse* (Unhappy India), Rieder.

12 March: Gandhi starts Dandi March.

4 May: Gandhi is arrested.

14 June: 'l'Inde vaincra', *Monde*.

20 June: Visit of Nag.

8 July: Visit of Raja Rao.

12 July: Visit of Rana.

28 August: Conversations with Tagore in Geneva, attended by R. Rao, A. Chakravarty and C. F. Andrews.

14 and 21 September: Visits of Nag.

19 September: Visit of J. C. Bose and Lady Bose.

First Round Table Conference in London.

1931   26 January: Gandhi is set free.

February: 'Europe, élargis-toi ou meurs! Réponse à Gaston Riou,' *Nouvelle Revue Mondiale 2*.

March: 'Three conversations. Tagore talks with
Einstein, with Rolland, and with Wells,'
Asia, XXXI

5 March: Gandhi-Irwin Pact signed.

April–May: 'Suite à: Europe, élargistoi ou
meurs!' *La Paix Mondiale*, 4.

Preface to the 'Vie de Gandhi, écrite par
lui-même,' *Europe, XXV*, and extracts in
L'Horizon, Brussels.

16 June: Death of Romain Rolland's father.

11 September: Madeleine Rolland and Edmond
Privat wecome Gandhi in Marseille.

Second Round Table Conference. Gandhi
sails for England in August, to attend the
Round Table Conference (September–
November) in London.

13 September: Visit of P. Seshadri.

6–11 December: Conversations between R.
Rolland and Gandhi at Villeneuve.

Gandhi returns to Bombay in December via
Villeneuve.

1932   January: Gandhi is arrested.

February: Letter to the editor in *India Bulletin*, I.

'Courriers de l'Inde' (*I, II, III*), in *Europe,
XXVIII* and *XXX*.

'Tagore et Gandhi pendant le jeûne,' *Europe,
XXX*.

17 April: Visits of D. C. Lall, Sh. Chetti, P. P.
Pillai, R. Rao.

27–9 August: World Congress against War in
Amsterdam, organized by R. Rolland and
Barbusse.

September: Gandhi's fast.

25 September: Poona Pact.

6 October: Pro Indian Assembly in Geneva.

'Le Christ des Indes'.

12 October: Visit of Swami Vijayananda.

13–14 October: Visit of Verrier Elwin.

23 October: Visit of M. H. Syed.

1 November: Visit of Dr Ansari.

1933	'Vers l'Unité de l'Inde par l'entente hindoue-musulmane,' *Europe, XXXI.*
	'Documents sur l'Inde' (*I, II*), in *Europe, XXXI-XXXII.*
	'Pour les condamnés de Meerut,' *Europe, XXXI.*
	3 February: Visit of A. Danielou.
	April: Romain Rolland refuses the Goethe Medal offered by Germany.
	30 January: Hitler Chancellor of Germany.
	February 1933: Gandhi starts the weekly *Harijan.*
	May: Gandhi arrested and released.
	June: Named honorary president of the World Committee against War and Fascism.
	August: Gandhi arrested and released.
	24 November: Conversations with Saumyendranath Tagore, later published in *The Modern Review, LVIII.*
1934	25 November: Visit of T. C. Khandwala.
	19 April: Visit of Dr. M. Sirker.
	28 April: Romain Rolland maries Marie Koudachev.
	July and December: Visits of Madeleine Slade.
1935	*Quinze ans de combat*, Rieder; *Par la revolution, la paix*, E.S.I.
	13 January: Visit of A. Chakravarty.
	April: Visit of Subhas Chandra Bose.
	19 May: Visit of Swami Yatiswarananda and Paul Geheeb.
	June–July: Trip to Russia, on the invitation of Gorki. Conversations with Stalin.
	22 January: Government of India Bill published.
	8 August: Visit of M. K. Nair.
	22 October: Visit of Nehru and his daughter Indira.
	2 August: Government of India Act receives royal assent.

1936	31 January: Celebration in Paris of the seventieth birthday of Romain Rolland.
	27 February: Visit of Subhas Chandra Bose.
	15 March: 'Interview with Aragon, '*Les cahiers du bolchevisme*.
	3 April: Visit of Miss MacLeod and Jean Herbert.
	Popular Front in France Spanish Civil War.
	4 December: 'Address to the Indian National Congress'.
1937	June: Visits of E. Horup, S. C Sen, Mr and Mrs Meta.
	20 June: Visit of Jean Herbert and Miss Reymont.
	28 July: Visit of A. Bose, nephew of Subhas Chandra Bose.
	15 October: Visit of Mahmoud uz Zafar Khan and his wife, Dr Rashid Jehan.
	Death of J.C. Bose.
1938	30 March: Visit of Jean Herbert and his wife, and Swami Siddeswarananda.
	8 June: Romain Rolland settles in Vézelay.
	30 September: Munich Accords.
	October: Protests against the Munich Accords.
	December: Visit of Jean Herbert. Romain Rolland begins writing his *Memoires*.
1939	February: 'Acte de reconnaissance d'un homme d' occident à Gandhi'.
	Protests against the invasion of Czechoslovakia.
	3 August: Visit of Chettiar.
	Hitler invades Czechoslovakia.
	23 August: German-Soviet Pact.
	Writes a letter of resignation from the Association of the Friends of the Soviet Union, after the signature of the Pact.
1939	3 September: Letter to President Daladier.
	Robespierre, Albin Michel.
1939–45	Word War II.

1940–4	Romain Rolland divides his time between Vézelay and Paris (89, bd. Montparnasse). Continues writing his *Memoires*, returns to the text of *Le Voyage Interieur*, Albin Michel (1942).
1940	Death of C. F. Andrews.
1941	Death of Tagore.
	Renews his friendship with Paul Claudel and Gillet; writes a long biography of Péguy writes *Entretiens sur les Evangiles*.
1944	30 December: Death of Romain Rolland. Buried at Brèves; his wife, Marie R. Rolland (1895–1985), also interred at Brèves.
1945	*Péguy*, Albin Michel.
1947	15 August: Independence of India.
1948	30 January: Gandhi is assassinated.

INDEX